Traveling the World
Through Your Favorite Movies

FILM + TRAVEL

NORTH AMERICA > SOUTH AMERICA

MUSEYON
GUIDES

M

A CURATED GUIDE TO YOUR OBSESSIONS

www.museyon.com

© Museyon, Inc. 2009

Publisher: Akira Chiba
Editor-in-Chief: Anne Ishii
Art Director: Alene Jackson
Production Manager: Michael Yong
Photography Editor: Michael Kuhle
Film Stills: Courtesy of Everett Collection

Permission to use *Vertigo* courtesy of: © 1958 Universal City Studios, Inc.
for Samuel Taylor and Patricia Hitchcock O'Connell as trustees
Cover Illustration: © Jillian Tamaki copyright 2008

Published in the United States by:
Museyon, Inc.
20 E. 46th St. Ste. 1400
New York, NY 10017

Museyon is a registered trademark.
Visit us online at www.museyon.com

ISBN 978-0-9822320-2-6

021061

Printed in China

CANADA

San Francisco,
California

UNITED STATES OF AMERICA

New York City,
New York

North Carolina
South Carolina
Georgia

Louisiana   Mississippi

MEXICO

PUERTO
RICO

CHILE

ARGENTINA

MAP : **NORTH AND SOUTH AMERICA**

TABLE OF CONTENTS

01 : HAUNTING AND BEAUTIFUL 9
SAN FRANCISCO, USA BY LIZ BROWN

02 : THE MANHATTAN PROJECT 27
NEW YORK CITY, USA BY NISHA GOPALAN

HAUNTING
AND BEAUTIFUL
SAN FRANCISCO, USA

LIZ BROWN
Most memorable experience in film/travel: Having spent some formative years in San Francisco, I'm always thrilled and terrified by the scene in *Vertigo* when Kim Novak throws herself into the Bay at Fort Point.

San Francisco Bay

Alcatraz

Embarcadero

Pacific Ocean

Golden Gate Bridge

Marina

Presidio

Pacific Heights

Treasure Island

Downtown

Bay Bridge

Golden Gate Park

Mission Dolores Park (The Mission district)

San Francisco

9

Maybe it's San Francisco's topography:

all those hills and peaks, the picturesque streets lined with brightly painted Victorian houses that suddenly give way to sheer, plummeting angles. Or maybe it's the climate. In San Francisco, there are days shot through with clear northern California light, and then there are days bound up in dense, clinging banks of fog. Whatever the reason, the men roaming the city streets are haunted. At least the ones on film are. Despite its reputation for Summer of Love-loving, Beat-living, rainbow flag-waving and all-around-cheerful eccentricity, the city has contributed to a startlingly large number of celluloid misfits and obsessives to the silver screen.

There is no question that the city is easy on the camera eye. So many films set here open with long panoramic shots, sweeping across postcard-famous vistas including Coit Tower, the Transamerica Pyramid, the Ferry Building, the Bay Bridge, Treasure Island, Alcatraz, the Embarcadero, the Marin Headlands and, of course, the Golden Gate Bridge. In some movies, the city may remain a mere backdrop, but San Francisco itself is usually an essential element of the drama, as if the people who settled and developed the land planned the streets specifically for chase scenes.

HARD-BOILED FILMS
FROM THE 1940s TO THE 1960s

The quintessential hard-boiled man in pursuit is Humphrey Bogart—brooding, smoking and slugging his way through the shadows as detective Sam Spade in *The Maltese Falcon* (1941). Based on the Dashiell Hammett novel and directed by John Huston, the film was produced mostly on studio sets in Los Angeles, but key scenes were shot on location. On **Burrit Alley,** just off Bush Street above the Stockton Tunnel, you can find a plaque indicating the spot where Spade's partner Miles Archer is killed.

˄ *The Maltese Falcon,* 1941. photo: ©Warner Bros./Everett Collection
˂ [previous page] **Lombard Street** photo: ©Aron Brand
[this page] **Transamerica Pyramid** photo: ©Jose Antonio Sanchez

In Delmer Daves' *Dark Passage* (1947), Bogart's Vincent Parry is both the hunter and hunted. Framed for his wife's murder, he escapes San Quentin prison to track down the real murderer and undergoes plastic surgery to disguise himself. He's also picked up and sheltered by the ever-sleek Lauren Bacall as Irene Jansen, an artist who fittingly lives in a fantastically stylish white art-deco confection at **1360 Montgomery Street** (at Filbert Street).

Maybe it's really quite simple: the manhunt is such a popular form for films set in San Francisco because it requires a large-scale tour of the city. From Bogart you can trace the lineage of the taciturn detective-on-the-trail to Steve McQueen's Frank Bullitt and Clint Eastwood's Harry Callahan. Hardened and cynical, they buck the system to bring mobsters, politicians and serial killers to justice. In *Bullitt* (1968), directed by Peter Yates,

McQueen is in search of the men who murdered a witness held in custody at the Hotel Daniels, (at the time the Kennedy Hotel) across from Pier 18. The elevated freeway that ran alongside the building was destroyed along with the hotel in the Loma Prieta earthquake of 1989. But many other key locations are still standing: **1153 Taylor Street**, where Bullitt lives, as well as the market across the street where he buys his TV dinners; **San Francisco General Hospital**; the **Grace Cathedral**, where the slimy pol played by Robert Vaughn serves papers to Bullitt's captain, at California and Taylor Streets on Nob Hill; the **Mark Hopkins Intercontinental Hotel**; and **Enrico's Sidewalk Cafe** at 504 Broadway, where Bullitt meets with an informant. The film's famous chase scene—which required two Mustangs and two Dodge Chargers—begins at **Portrero** and **Army** streets, races through Bernal Heights, and manages to jump between the Russian Hill and North Beach neighborhoods, the Portrero Hills, and the Marina, veering past **Saints Peter and Paul Church**, **Bimbo's 365**, **Fort Mason** and the **Marina Safeway** before the big explosion along the southbound **Guadalupe Canyon Parkway**.

^ *Bullitt,* 1963. photo: ©Warner Bros./Everett Collection
‹ **Grace Cathedral** photo: ©Can Balcioglu
[next page] **Golden Gate Park** photo: ©Chee-Onn Leong

THE ZODIAC KILLINGS, THEN AND NOW

Directed by Don Siegel, *Dirty Harry* (1971) was inspired in part by the real-life Zodiac killings in the late '60s and the efforts of detective Dave Toschi, one of the investigators on the still-unsolved case. Clint Eastwood's portrayal of Harry Callahan—blunt, hard-edged, squinting—would become an iconic persona. Whether apprehending a bank robber while holding a hot dog or pursuing the baby-faced psychopath "Scorpio" (as played by Andy Robinson), Callahan roams the city far and wide. The existing landmarks featured include the **Hall of Justice** at 850 Bryant Street, the **Marina Boat Docks**, the **Portrero Hills**, the **Mount Davidson Cross** above Portola Drive, **City Hall**, **Kezar Stadium** and the buffalo paddock in **Golden Gate Park**. The final showdown's rock quarry in Marin County, however, has since been turned into the Larkspur Landing Shopping Center.

David Fincher's *Zodiac* (2007) revisited the events of the actual murders, and in his incredibly fetishistic recreation of 1970s San Francisco, there are three men on the case: Mark Ruffalo's Toschi, Jake Gyllenhaal's cartoonist Robert Graysmith and Robert Downey, Jr. as a crime reporter. While Fincher shot many of the film's interiors in Los Angeles, the Bay Area native, with a reputation for punishing exactitude, insisted on shooting at the precise locations of the Zodiac attacks, such as **Lake Berryessa**—which meant building an entire irrigation system and replanting 24 trees, plus a thousand clumps of grass, to replicate the area's earlier scenery.

THE *VERTIGO* TOUR

And then there's the obsessive of all obsessives: Jimmy Stewart's John "Scottie" Ferguson in *Vertigo* (1958). Riven by phobia, fantasy and fetish, he lusts for Kim Novak's glamorous Madeleine Elster while cruelly remaking her counterpart, the plain, always-yielding Judy. A "womanhunt," Alfred Hitchcock's film uses the city's vertiginous, winding streets to reinforce the suspense and foreboding of Scottie's growing psychosis. A devoted fan can tour many key locations, starting with the upscale **Brocklebank Apartments** at 100 Mason Street, where Madeleine lives. There is no portrait of Carlotta Valdes at the **Palace of the Legion of Honor**,

but you can visit the museum in Lincoln Park. Nor is there an actual grave for Carlotta in the cemetery behind the **Mission Dolores** at 320 Dolores Street, though one stone does exist to commemorate the thousands of indigenous people who died after Spanish missionaries occupied the region. Dolores Street is also the site of the oldest building in the city, Mission San Francisco de Asís, completed in 1791. Just beneath the Golden Gate Bridge at the northwest edge of the city lies **Fort Point**. Built in the 1850s, it's where Madeleine takes her suicidal leap into the crashing waves of the Bay, and Scottie soon follows. Take a pass by **900 Lombard Street** at the base of those famed hairpin turns to see Scottie's apartment where he brings Madeleine after fishing her out of the water. Other significant spots, such as the red-walled Ernie's Restaurant or the McKittrick Hotel, no longer remain, but you can stop in at what was **Hotel Empire**, Judy's low-rent lodging at 940 Sutter Street, which is currently the York Hotel and will be renamed Hotel Vertigo upon completion of its renovation.

MOVIE PANIC AND PARANOIA

Perhaps less imposing—but no less driven—than the iconic characters played by Stewart, Eastwood, McQueen and Bogart is Gene Hackman's buttoned-down, uncharismatic Harry Caul in *The Conversation* (1974). Francis Ford Coppola's unsettling plunge into the world of surveillance and spiraling paranoia opens on **Union Square** where Harry and his partner Stan (John Cazale) are huddled in a van on Geary Street, listening in on a young couple's conversation. The City of Paris department store is gone now, replaced by Neiman Marcus. Other critical scenes take place in the then-newly erected **Embarcadero One** and outside the **Maritime Plaza**. It is in the **Jack Tar Hotel**, now the Cathedral Hotel, that Harry makes his final attempt at surveillance.

Of course men are not the only ones who succumb to dangerous fixations in San Francisco. While most of Hitchcock's *The Birds* (1963) was shot either on studio lots or on location up the coast at **Bodega Bay**, the film begins with Tippie Hedren's socialite Melanie Daniels making her fateful purchase

of a pair of lovebirds at a pet store on **Powell Street**, just across the way from where Harry Caul sets up his first spy operation in Union Square.

And certainly Zasu Pitts' Trina Sieppe is a woman possessed in Erich von Stroheim's *Greed* (1924), a silent film tour de force that was butchered by studio editors. A four-hour version of the once nine-hour film has since been reconstructed. Based on Frank Norris' novel *McTeague*, the movie follows the travails of an unlicensed dentist (Gibson Gowland) and his wife, who wins the lottery; her lust for gold comes to know no bounds. In one incredible scene, the wraithlike, kohl-eyed Pitts slithers against her pile of coins under the bed covers with total sexual glee. Von Stroheim shot much of the movie on location, including the Sierra Nevada mountains, Death Valley, and the corner of **Hayes and Laguna streets**, which is the site of McTeague's dental office.

HAPPIER EVER AFTER

As von Stroheim clearly saw, and as plenty of gold miners and dotcom entrepreneurs have come to know all too well, San Francisco was built on cycles of boom and bust. Today, though, that particular narrative about sudden change of fortune is not a gimlet-eyed account of hoarding and rapaciousness, but a heart-warming tale of overcoming adversity in Gabriele Muccino's *The Pursuit of Happyness* (2006). As Will Smith plays him, Chris Gardner, a homeless optimist and struggling single father, manages to leap from his unpaid internship at Dean Witter to starting his own brokerage firm, ultimately selling it at a multimillion-dollar profit. This particular American Dream, based on a true story, plays out at such locations as the **Glide Memorial Church** on Ellis Street and **555 California Street**, the former Bank of America headquarters and the very skyscraper that the "Scorpio" killer shoots one of his victims in *Dirty Harry*.

In spite of being host to *The Lady From Shanghai* (1947), *The Towering Inferno* (1974) and *Invasion of the Body Snatchers* (1978), the city has been the site of plenty of light-hearted pictures. One movie that takes bizarro quirk to staggering heights is Otto Preminger's cult film *Skidoo* (1968), a fascinating, candy-colored collision of hippies and squares, featuring Carol Channing, Frankie Avalon, Mickey Rooney, Groucho Marx and Jackie Gleason. (The latter sneaks into the prison on **Alcatraz** where he ends up having a deliriously mind-blowing acid trip.) Other merry adventures by the

> **Palace of Fine Arts** photo: ©Andy Z

Bay feature Woody Allen relocating his usual New York neuroses in *Play It Again, Sam* (1972) and Whoopi Goldberg going undercover in *Sister Act* (1992). Although whatever fuels resident Robin Williams (a.k.a. Mrs. Doubtfire and Patch Adams) in his comic mania, it's probably not exactly free-flowing ebullient joy but something much murkier.

And finally, take the story of the huge and hugely popular Fatty Arbuckle. Thanks to YouTube you can see his jolly plump face and take in the city circa 1915 in *Mabel and Fatty Viewing the World's Fair at San Francisco*. (The **Palace of Fine Arts**, another *Vertigo* location, is the one remaining structure from the Panama-Pacific International Exposition.) Six years later, at the height of his fame, Arbuckle was back in San Francisco hosting a party at the **St. Francis Hotel** when he allegedly raped Virginia Rappe, an aspiring actress who died from a ruptured bladder two days later. Arbuckle was tried three separate times and ultimately acquitted. His career never recovered. There probably isn't a plaque at the hotel commemorating the sordid event, but the party was reported to have been in room 1220. (A curious side note: Before he was a famous novelist, Dashiell Hammett worked for the Pinkerton Agency as a private investigator, where one of his cases was this very scandal.)

So what is it about all those glorious panoramas? Why are the men and women of San Francisco's screenscape so driven and so dark? Maybe knowing that beneath that breathtaking landscape—staggering hills, an expansive coastline, a sprawling bay, that spectacular bridge—the earth, or more specifically the North American Plate, is always in motion, always sliding, always grinding against the Pacific Plate, will do that to you. §

Liz Brown has written about movies and movie stars for publications such as *Bookforum*, the *London Review of Books*, the *Los Angeles Times*, and *The New York Times Book Review*.

∧ *Skidoo*, 1968. photo: ©Otto Preminger Films/Everett Collection
‹ **St. Francis Hotel** photo: ©Dana Tuszke
[next page] **Manhattan Skyline** photo: ©bravobravo

02

THE MANHATTAN PROJECT
NEW YORK CITY, USA

NISHA GOPALAN
Most memorable experience in film/travel: I hope she never sees this, but my sweet, kind, doting aunt in Bombay was a member of India's film censorship board—which, with all due respect, I consider absolutely mortifying.

Upper West Side

Central Park

Upper East Side

QUEENS

MANHATTAN

Times Sq

Hudson River

Midtown

East River

Union Square

Greenwich Village

East Village

BROOKLYN

New York City

Tribeca

Downtown

For roughly one year in the 18th century (1789–1790, to be exact), New York City was the capital of America ... before Philly and then D.C. nicked that honor. But what it ultimately lacked in civic distinction, the borough of Manhattan more than made up for in vitality. Because somewhere between the 1620s, when the Dutch ponied up just 24 bucks to buy the land from Native Americans (unpaved highway robbery!), and the turn-of-the-century industrial era, when the subway sprawled and immigrants abounded, this former Revolutionary War stomping ground swelled into a booming metropolis. Unimpressed, English author Rudyard Kipling once described the Big Apple as the "shiftless outcome of squalid barbarism and reckless extravagance"–and indeed, it's proven an inspiration to many an artist, whether awed or disgusted by the unruly setting before them.

In recent years, sentimentalists have lamented the glossier, safer NYC, a locale far removed from the crime-ridden, hedonistic, art-stoking '70s or the '80s, during which a crack epidemic, the AIDS crisis and bombastic Wall Street glitz curiously coexisted. Despite the grousing, this protean city has remained fertile ground for thought. And so it's here—at the crossroads of infatuation and skepticism—that we lead you on a tour of NYC-set films that have proved decade-spanning cultural markers of this urban playground's persistent relevance.

DOWNTOWN

The mistaken-identity antics of *Desperately Seeking Susan* (1985), Susan Seidelman's benign paean to East Village postpunk bohemia, begins in a thrift store where Madonna hawks her one-of-a-kind jacket—the awesome one with a gold pyramid on the back—that's

later picked-up at **Love Saves the Day** (119 Second Ave., between 7th St. and St. Mark's Place) by hausfrau/Madonna-wannabe Rosanna Arquette.

If '70s soul is more your thing, head to the West Village's still-standing **Café Reggio** (119 Macdougal St., between Minetta and 3rd St.), immortalized in the like-titled instrumental on Isaac Hayes' soundtrack to *Shaft* (1971). The restaurant, which declares itself the home of America's first cappuccino maker, is where Richard Roundtree's "black private dick that's a sex machine to all the chicks" (you're damn right!) meets up with an associate, then winds up taking a bullet in his badass shoulder.

While you're here, you may as well move along to TriBeCa (or, the Triangle Below Canal Street). The former home to John F. Kennedy, Jr. and preferred hood of Robert De Niro, this nabe housed the *Ghostbusters*

(1984) headquarters, better known as **Hook & Ladder Company #8** (a fully functioning firehouse at 14 North Moore St, between Varick and West Broadway). Also in the area: a parking lot at West Broadway and North Moore where that ridiculous "freak gasoline fight accident" goes down in *Zoolander* (2001), leaving Ben Stiller's pouty character as its only survivor.

TOWARDS MIDTOWN

After Vito Corleone survives an assassination attempt in *The Godfather* (1972), good son Michael visits him at an infirmary, shrewdly orchestrating a bait and switch there in anticipation of another attempt on his dad's life. (The interior hospital shots actually take place near the East Village at **The New York Eye and Ear Infirmary**, at 310 East 14th St., between First and Second Ave.) Outside, at the **Bellevue Hospital Center** (462 First Ave., between 26th and 28th Streets)—the oldest public hospital in America—he gets a knuckle sandwich after confronting no-good cop Captain McCluskey, who's clearly on a rival's payroll. Oh, that knave will get his later! Michael

crosses over to the Dark Side when he guns down McCluskey and the boss who tried to whack the Don over pasta and vino at the dearly departed Luna restaurant in the Bronx.

Remember halter-topped Marilyn Monroe's notorious encounter with a drafty subway grate, to publisher Tom Ewell's delight, in *The Seven Year Itch* (1955)? Well, that would be a street-level vent located in front of the **Trans-Lux 52nd Street Theater** (586 Lexington at 52nd St.). However, if you can't find it, don't despair: The artsy movie house has long since closed, but you can still find the grate which, alas, does not huff and puff as much as you were led to believe.

Continue uptown along the East River and you'll likely notice the picture-postcard view off **Riverview Terrace** at Sutton Square (just beneath the 59th Street/Queensboro Bridge between Sutton Place and FDR Dr.). This is where Woody Allen's Isaac Davis and his best friend's mistress, portrayed by Diane Keaton, sit on a bench and watch the sunrise in *Manhattan* (1979)—a scene featured on that movie's lovely poster. The film, incidentally, opens on the Upper East Side at present-day power-lunch hangout **Elaine's** (1703 Second Avenue between 88th and 89th); there, our neurotic protagonist itemizes the expenses of dating a 17-year-old, played by Mariel Hemingway. (We'll pause while you contemplate the scene's prescience with respect to the director's real love life.) The teen later dumps him at the original **John's Pizzeria** (278 Bleecker Street between Jones and Morton streets), purported by Allen and many, many others to make the finest pizza pie in New York City.

The fabulous wedding that almost never was, between fashionista Carrie Bradshaw (Sarah Jessica Parker) and publishing-bigwig–turned–vineyard-proprietor Mr. Big (Chris Noth) in the *Sex and the City* movie (2008), goes down ever-so-bathetically at the main branch of the stately **New York Public Library** (Fifth Ave. and 42nd St.)—and then plays out further on Fifth Ave. Apparently the building is a veritable harbinger of doom, it also being the haunted library at the start of *Ghostbusters*.

The Honeymooners, The Merv Griffin Show, The Late Show With David Letterman—all have shot at the **Ed Sullivan Theater** (1697 Broadway between 53rd and 54th streets), made famous by the seminal talk-show host. But the theater got edgy when it cameo'd in *Taxi Driver* (1976). At a pay phone nearby, De Niro's misfit vet Travis Bickle calls Cybill Shepherd's fetching

> **Times Square** photo: ©William Warby

Betsy to awkwardly apologize for taking her to an adult film in Times Square—at the presently demolished **Lyric Theater** (213 West 42nd St., between Seventh and Eighth avenues, currently the Hilton Theater)—on their first and only date. Want to complete the Martin Scorsese/*Taxi Driver* on-screen theater trifecta? Head down to Union Square, the former site of the **Variety Theater** (110 Third Ave., between 13th and 14th streets). Jodie Foster's Iris, an underage prostitute, jumps into Bickle's cab here before her buff no-BS pimp, played by Harvey Keitel, drags her back out onto the street.

CENTRAL PARK ADJACENT

At the south tip of NYC's great park, you'll find **The Plaza Hotel** (Fifth Ave. at Central Park South), the majestic, just-renovated site of Michael Douglas and Catherine Zeta-Jones' disgustingly lavish nuptials in 2000. Movie buffs may recognize the landmark from an early scene in *North by Northwest* (1959) that nudges the Alfred Hitchcock thriller into action: It's here, in the fabled Oak Bar, that foxy Cary Grant is abducted after being mistaken for a government spook. Way less prestigiously, the lodging is also where outback-Aussie Mick Dundee takes his first bubble bath in *Crocodile Dundee* (1986).

Across the street stands the giant **FAO Schwarz** flagship store (767 Fifth Ave. at 58th St.), made famous by Tom Hanks and Robert Loggia in *Big* (1988) where they play an impromptu duet of "Heart and Soul" on the toy store's giant floor-piano.

Travel about a dozen blocks up the west side of the park and you'll see **The Dakota** (1 West 72nd St. at Central Park West). The site of John Lennon and Yoko Ono's residence as well as the ex-Beatles' murder in 1980, it previously served as the digs in *Rosemary's Baby* (1968) where the innocent, pixie-haired, pregnant Mia Farrow nests with her on-screen husband John Cassavetes—unaware of the hellish birth that awaits her.

And just seven blocks up from there, the cast of *The Devil Wears Prada* (2006) shot the benefit scene—you know, in which the once-dowdy Anne Hathaway provides crucial back-up to a snappy, sniffling Emily Blunt—at **The American Museum of Natural History** (Central Park West at 79th St.). Venture south a bit and you can check out the **McGraw Hill** building (1221 Avenue of the Americas, between 48th and 49th St.), site of Elias-

Clark publishing, where our conflicted heroine works. In *Malcolm X* (1992), meanwhile, the black activist enjoys a first date with future wife Betty Shabazz, played by Angela Bassett, at the Natural History museum. The tragic end of Spike Lee's epic takes place at the still-standing—if radically altered—**Audubon Business and Technology Center** (3940 Broadway between 165th and 166th streets, up the island of Manhattan in Washington Heights). Formerly the Audubon Ballroom, it's the same spot where the real Malcolm X was suddenly gunned down while giving a speech for the Organization of Afro-American Unity. Interior shots for that scene take place at the now-extinct **Hotel Diplomat** in Times Square (108 West 43rd between Broadway and Sixth Ave.).

MIDTOWN TO UPTOWN

A hoity-toity symbol of old-school wealth and the gilded life, **The Waldorf-Astoria** hotel (100 East 50th St., at Park Ave.) is a storied location. Its occupants have included electricity whiz Nikola Tesla, musician Cole

Porter, gangster Bugsy Siegel, and innumerable diplomats and world leaders. Heck, the place even has a *salad* named after it. Which is ostensibly why Wes Anderson, director of *The Royal Tenenbaums* (2001), chose the institution to play the part of the WASPy Lindbergh Palace Hotel in his picture about a broke patriarch (Gene Hackman) who's ousted from this longtime residence—and kicked out of his dejected kids' lives.

The Waldorf is to hotels what **Tiffany & Co.** (727 Fifth Ave., between 56th and 57th streets), immortalized by the graceful Audrey Hepburn in *Breakfast at Tiffany's* (1961), is to jewelers. Interesting then that *Midnight Cowboy* (1969) chooses the grande dame of all things exquisite as the setting to introduce Jon Voight's future gigolo, the fresh-off-the-bus Joe Buck, to the concrete jungle. A block up and a few avenues over (58th St. and Fifth Ave.), Dustin Hoffman's limping urchin, Ratzo Rizzo, later imparts some streetwise wisdom to the naïve Mr. Buck. He's interrupted by a reckless, impatient cabbie and famously yells, "I'm walking here! I'm walking here!"

What would a tour of New York be with out a shout-out to one of its most iconic films ... even if most of its environs are AWOL? *Annie Hall* is a lingering, loving tour of Woody Allen's hometown, and one of its most memorable scenes occurs on the Upper East Side at the old **Beekman Cinema** (1254 Second Ave. between 65th and 66th streets). While waiting for Diane Keaton's stylish, titular character to arrive for a movie date, Allen's uptight comedian, Alvy Singer, is harassed by an annoying, autograph-seeking fan. At the film's wistful end, Alvy bumps into Annie with her new beau at the also-gone **Thalia Cinema** (250 West 95th St. between Amsterdam and Broadway)—which later became the Symphony Space/Leonard Nimoy Thalia Theater, thanks to its benefactor, Spock! Coincidentally, Annie and her man were seeing a film called *The Sorrow and the Pity*.

It's fitting to complete your Gotham tour with a look back at *The Warriors* (1979). A menacing flick at its time, today it plays almost like a dystopian science fiction play in its extreme depictions of gang upheaval in New York City—especially considering what a candy-coated wonderland the city is now. The drama begins in **Van Cortlandt Park** (which starts near 242nd St. and Broadway, past Manhattan in the Bronx) where various factions assemble for an ill-fated summit—sort of like in *The Godfather*, only with coordinated and chest-exposing wardrobe. The Warriors subsequently throw down with the Baseball Furies—and win!—after entering their rivals' territory at the **72nd St. subway station** (72nd and Broadway) on the Upper West Side and running past Fireman's Monument (100th St. and Riverside Dr.) into **Riverside Park** (Riverside Dr., roughly between West 80th and 99th streets). Today the latter boasts free kayaking, wi-fi, and a cavalcade of cyclists wearing inappropriately tight spandex. A travesty? Perhaps. But as cinema can attest, New York City is always in flux, which is what makes it such a conflicting, charging, complicated muse. §

Nisha Gopalan has been living in New York City since 1996. She's previously been a writer at the late *Premiere* magazine, and more recently an editor at *Entertainment Weekly*.

∧ *Annie Hall*, 1977. photo: ©Rollins-Joffe Productions/Everett Collection
< **Riverside Park** photo: ©Christopher Walker
[next page] **Porch swing** photo: ©Terrie L. Zeller

AN IMAGINARY SOUTH

SOUTHERN USA

MEAKIN ARMSTRONG
Most memorable experience in film/travel: My MFA qualifies me to either teach film or manage any video store in the country but I've never taken advantage of either.

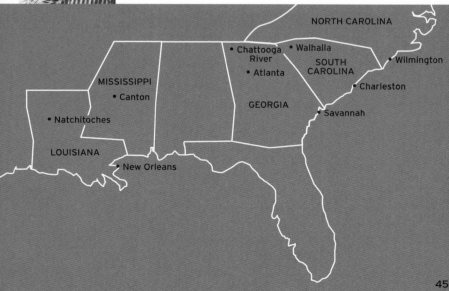

NORTH CAROLINA

Chattooga River • Walhalla

SOUTH CAROLINA

• Atlanta

• Wilmington

MISSISSIPPI

• Canton

• Charleston

GEORGIA

• Natchitoches

• Savannah

LOUISIANA

• New Orleans

Fried chicken and sweet tea. The sound of a

genteel accent. Someone wilting in the heat and humidity. The
Civil War. Flashes of deviance, wild passion, extreme violence.
All are tied-up in the mythology of the American South. Here,
the combination of poverty and wounded Confederate pride—
not to mention the tragedy of Jim Crow—yielded a cultural
landscape unlike any other. This landscape is the inspiration for
countless memorable lines, such as, "Frankly, my dear, I don't
give a damn" and "I have always depended upon the kindness
of strangers."

Much of the filmic South, however, isn't Southern at all. *Gone with the Wind*
(1939), sacred to many below the Mason-Dixon Line, was shot entirely in
California. And its leading lady, Vivien Leigh, wasn't even American, but
British. When Leigh later starred in *A Streetcar Named Desire* (1951), she
and Marlon Brando worked mostly on a soundstage. The "realism" of 1967's
In the Heat of the Night was contrived in small-town Illinois. As for TV's
The Andy Griffith Show, a noted celebrant of the quieter aspects of the
down-home lifestyle? It was shot on the same back lot as *GWTW*, with the
abandoned Tara Plantation set rotting just up the hill from Mayberry.

One could justifiably wonder if the South only
exists as a construct of directors and novelists:
the dozens of businesses and individuals
named after fictional characters, such as
Scarlett, Rhett, and Tara can lead one to think
so. Enough people seem to view the imaginary
South as actual history that the sextant at one
of the old-line church cemeteries in Charleston,
South Carolina used to point at a damaged,
unreadable gravestone, and say: "There lies
Rhett Butler." Of course Rhett never existed,
but as a well-heeled ne'er-do-well from an
aristocratic background, he is an archetype of
the region, especially Charleston—as are permutations of the always-polite
Melanie Wilkes, the out-of-towner Mr. Tibbs, the tough talking beauty-shop
steel magnolia, or even the manipulative Scarlett O'Hara herself.

^ **Gone With The Wind,** 1939. photo: ©Warner Bros./Everett Collection
< **Mansion, New Orleans** photo: ©Natalia Bratslavsky

A large part of living in the South is living with the tragedy of the past. Race relations are an unavoidable issue here, despite the great amount of progress made. After all, not too long ago, this is where gross governmental neglect allowed the African-American community of New Orleans to suffer and die in the Superdome, as seen on televisions everywhere and in Spike Lee's *When the Levees Broke* (2006).

ATLANTA, GEORGIA

The South has changed and is changing still—it's home to a highly successful black-owned film studio (Tyler Perry Studios is located in southwestern Atlanta), and increasingly, films are being made about the South in an honest and forthcoming way. In several of its cities, African-Americans also hold leadership positions. **Atlanta** is often cited as an example of a place where blacks and whites are reinventing their relationship and thereby reinventing the South as a whole. Atlanta is also the logical starting point of any tour of the South—it's the de facto capital. Currently festooned with glass towers and highways, it's the birthplace of *Gone With the Wind* author Margaret Mitchell, whose former home, the **Margaret Mitchell House & Museum**, has among its possessions the front door to Tara and the portrait of Scarlett O'Hara, both lifted from the movie set. The painting of Scarlett, as seen in Rhett's house, still bears a liquor stain from the drink that Rhett Butler (played by Clark Gable) threw at it.

Twice Mitchell's home has, for reasons unknown, been a victim of arson. Perhaps that's because the author's work is now controversial for avoiding issues of slavery and racism. *Driving Miss Daisy* (1989), however, would touch on the region's dark history, using a home on **Lullwater Road** in Druid Hills as a location for Daisy Werthan's house. This privileged district, with its multimillion-dollar residences—such as the one on Springdale Road built by the man who designed the Coke bottle—were ideal for dramatizing the economic disparity between the white Miss Daisy (Jessica Tandy) and her African-American driver, Hoke Colburn (Morgan Freeman).

Since the end of segregation, Atlanta has become one of the fastest growing cities in the developed world. *Sharkey's Machine* (1981), a gritty and underrated film directed by and starring Burt Reynolds, shows Atlanta bursting in all directions. The '80s were a transitional time for the area, since the "new" South was still emerging from the old. Much of what's visible

‹ **Centennial Park View, Atlanta** photo: ©jackweichen_gatech
[next page] **Forsyth Park Fountain, Savannah** photo: ©David Davis

in the background for *Sharkey* is lost, but the hotel where they filmed that record-breaking, 220-foot free fall from the **Westin Peachtree Plaza** exists. Stand on the street, look up, and see how hard that daring stuntman would've needed to push to hit the water.

Because of its size, many dissociate Atlanta from the South; it's as though the location of the sprawling metropolis were an accident of geography and nothing more. Southerners, like Talmudic scholars, often argue about which areas below the Mason-Dixon Line are truly a part of Dixie. What side did they fight for in the Civil War? Kentucky, Maryland and West Virginia wouldn't qualify. How many Yankees have taken over the area? Vast parts of Florida and Virginia, therefore, lose out. Even New Orleans is considered dubious, for being too freewheeling—too *French*.

SAVANNAH, GEORGIA

Self-appointed scholars of the region probably all agree that **Savannah** is integral to the Southland holy writ. Known for its hospitality and charm, this port city lies on the Intracoastal Waterway and is graced with miles of stately homes. Savannah has a rich antebellum history, but for over a decade, it has been best known as the site of the infamous '81 murder recounted in the best-seller–turned–film *Midnight in the Garden of Good and Evil* (1997).

A primer on the Southern penchant for gothic behavior, *Midnight* still lures visitors to Savannah. And it's possible to see many of the locations featured in the movie, such as **Club One** (where Lady Chablis occasionally performs) and the **Mercer House**, site of the killing, on Monterey Square. (Incidentally, the house was also in the 1989 movie *Glory*.) Nearby you'll find **Bonaventure Cemetery**—that's where Miss Minerva (Irma P. Hall) uttered her incantations.

> ∧ *Midnight in the Garden of Good and Evil,* 1997. photo: ©Warner Bros./Everett Collection
> ⟩ **Mercer House** photo: ©Laszlo A. Lim

Savannah's historic district is made up of 21 squares that vary in size and personality. Some are formal, with fountains and monuments, others are so small they're basically playgrounds. (Three additional squares were lost during the 1950s and '60s and may eventually be restored.) In **Chippewa Square**, Tom Hanks sat on a bench for 1994's *Forrest Gump* and ate his box of chocolates. That bench was a prop, but it can be visited at the **Savannah History Museum**, where it's on permanent display.

SOUTH CAROLINA

Charleston, also an antebellum jewel, is in many ways a rival to Savannah. But the South Carolina city wins the competition when it comes to real-world history. Off the tip of its peninsula, at a place called the Battery, troops fired upon Fort Sumter and started the Civil War. Located at the junction of the Ashley and Cooper Rivers, Charleston—perhaps the most aristocratic city of the South—has a sprawling historic district packed with colonial homes. In *Gone With the Wind*, it's the hometown of Rhett Butler ("He's from Charleston. He has the most terrible reputation."), to which he returns after abandoning Scarlett ("I'm going back to Charleston, back where I belong").

The College of Charleston, founded in 1770, is a frequent location choice for moviemakers. Located downtown, its campus flows seamlessly into the surrounding city. In fact, many of the college's administrative buildings are former homes. This downtown locale—peppered with antebellum mansions

and, on nearby **King Street**, charming shops— provided a backdrop for colonial thriller *The Patriot* (2000), the Civil War drama *Cold Mountain* (2003) and the contemporary romance *The Notebook* (2004). Additional scenes in *The Notebook* were filmed at **Boone Hall Plantation**, just outside the city. The estate is one of several plantations in the Charleston area that can be visited by the public, and it's easy to imagine that it was the inspiration for **Twelve Oaks**, the home of *Gone With the Wind*'s gentleman waffler, Ashley Wilkes. The ancient trees at Twelve Oaks were produced through artifice and special

﹀ *The Notebook,* 2004. photo: ©New Line/Everett Collection
‹ **King Street, Charleston** photo: ©Simply Living
[next page] **Chattooga River** photo: ©L Barnwell

effects, but Boone Hall has a genuine **Avenue of Oaks**, a three-quarter-mile-long row of trees approaching the plantation house. While there, be sure to visit the slave quarters—occupied by sharecroppers into the twentieth century—for a vantage point of the Southern past that is decidedly at odds with romantic puffery.

Charleston is the capital of the South Carolina Low country—an often-marshy coastal spot seen in *The Prince of Tides* (1991) and *The Big Chill* (1983). The Low country includes unspoiled **Edisto Island**, a picturesque locale featuring a peaceful beach dotted with seashells, some of the state's tallest palmetto trees, and a maritime live oak forest known for its gnarled branches dripping with Spanish moss. Look for it in *Ace Ventura: When Nature Calls* (1995), *The Patriot*, and *The Notebook*.

The foothills of the Appalachian Mountains along the South Carolina and Georgia border are one of the South's most famous locations. It's where director John Boorman filmed 1972's *Deliverance*. The **Chattooga River**,

where much of the drama takes place, is an official National Wild and Scenic River, with Sumter National Forest on the South Carolina banks and Chattahoochee National Forest on the Georgia side. The Chattooga is a 50-mile stretch of wilderness and one of the southeast's few remaining free-flowing streams. Once a little-known body of water, it has attracted many attempting to navigate the same route traveled by *Deliverance*'s Burt Reynolds, Jon Voight and Ned Beatty. Large portions of the film were shot on the part of the river called **Woodall Shoals**, located due west of a town called Walhalla. Much of the Chattooga is safe for canoeing, though the rapids at Woodall Shoals are very dangerous.

MISSISSIPPI

Small-town life is intrinsic to Southern living: it's the setting of the church supper, sweet-tea sipping and a slower pace. In the tiny towns of Dixie, the past isn't as easily paved over. **Canton** has increasingly become the

^ *Deliverance,* 1972. photo: ©Warner Bros./Everett Collection
> **Charleston, NC** photo: ©catnap72

quintessential small Southern town, thanks to appearances in *Thieves Like Us* (1974), *Mississippi Burning* (1988), *A Time to Kill* (1996), *My Dog Skip* (2000) and *O Brother, Where Art Thou?* (2000). The central square, built around a pristine 1827 Greek Revival courthouse, gives Canton a picture-perfect, Mayberry appeal. The city, in turn, preserves its cinematic heritage with the **Canton film museums** at which sets have been preserved.

NORTH CAROLINA

Wilmington, found on North Carolina's **Cape Fear Coast**, boasts a historic district (with neighborhoods ideal for strolling) that's one of the largest in U.S., according to the National Register of Historic Places. It also ranks third among American film-production sites, after Hollywood and New York City. A great many movies have been made around the city, on its soundstages and at nearby **Wrightsville Beach** and **Carolina Beach**—from *The Divine Secrets of the Ya-Ya Sisterhood* (2002) to *Nights in Rodanthe* (2008) and *The Secret Life of Bees* (2008). Even years after *Dawson's Creek* (1998–2003) left the air, the TV show continues to inspire a steady stream of visitors in search of spots where the series was filmed, many still standing and open to the public.

NATCHITOCHES, LOUISIANA

The portrayal of the typical Southerner has evolved from the early days of film through the present. In former times, white folks dithered among their ghosts and bric-a-brac while African-Americans waited on them as humble servants. The prior spoke poetically of loss and degradation, often in long paragraphs. In the modern paradigm, roles for African-Americans are still evolving—and with the rise of Tyler Perry and others, they will continue to. However, for the Southern white woman in particular, the change is obvious. She is now plainspoken and less patient with elision and delicacy. She is no longer a wan Vivien Leigh, but a Sandra Bullock or Julia Roberts, fighting the pressure to be always polite.

Along with 1991's *Fried Green Tomatoes* ("You know what we need instead of this baloney? Assertiveness training for Southern women. But that's a contradiction in terms, isn't it?"), 1989's *Steel Magnolias* played a major part in this filmic sea change. Shot entirely in **Natchitoches** (pronounced NAK-uh-tush) and written by a local resident, the movie is an anthem to the South and its women. Visitors can still find many of the locations used

in *Magnolias*, such as the **Henry Cook-Taylor House** (now the Steel Magnolia Bed and Breakfast) where Drum and M'Lynn Eatenton (Tom Skerritt and Sally Field) lived and the **American Cemetery** where Shelby (Julia Roberts) was buried. The oldest permanent settlement within the borders of the Louisiana Purchase, the area is dotted with Creole plantation homes, and its entire 33-block downtown district is a designated National Historic Landmark. Natchitoches Parish is also where John Wayne and William Holden filmed *The Horse Soldiers* in 1959.

In some ways, film preserves the South and keeps its myths at the forefront of the American imagination—for both better and worse. It has romanticized the slave era but also demonized Jim Crow. It reminds Southerners of their history, and what sets them apart—even if that so-called history is propaganda or fiction. Many of its stock characters are also clichés—the pot-bellied and cruel police chief and toothless backwoods yahoo are but two examples. No doubt, the steel magnolia will soon join them in that netherworld of the forgotten, replaced by a new paradigm. Clichés, after all, are just tired ideas that have outlived their usefulness. The South requires new characters and new movies shot in new locations because it is an ever-changing place under pressure to change even more. As Hollywood leaves the backlot and moves deeper into Dixie, one hopes it will help the South to continue to thrive in both myth and reality, and bring about an even better South. §

Meakin Armstrong is fiction editor of Guernica (guernicamag.com) and a freelance writer working on his first novel. He is additionally a contributor to the anthology *New York Calling: From Blackout to Bloomberg* (Reaktion/University of Chicago Press). Among the awards and grants he's received is a 2007 fiction scholarship to the Bread Loaf Writers' Conference.

^ *Steel Magnolias*, 1989. photo: ©TriStar Pictures/Everett Collection
< **Oak Alley Plantation, SC** photo: ©Jason Major

04

FILM
AND REALITY
MEXICO CITY, MEXICO

ENRIQUE RAMIREZ
Most memorable experience in film/travel: In 2007, I got a chance to visit Hans Scharoun's Berlin Stadtbibliothek, the library depicted in Wim Wenders' *Wings of Desire*. It was magical.

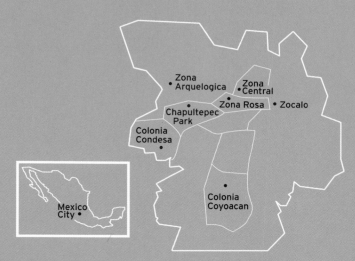

Zona Arquelogica

Zona Central

Zona Rosa

Zocalo

Chapultepec Park

Colonia Condesa

Colonia Coyoacan

Mexico City

"Mexico City is about to EXPLODE!"

If this tagline sounds familiar, then you probably saw the U.S. promotional materials for *Akira*, Katshuhiro Otomo's 1988 film adaptation of his critically-acclaimed manga. The line could apply equally well to the city's precarious location, in a caldera flanked by two volcanoes, and its booming film industry.

Mexico City has enjoyed a growing presence on the world stage of late thanks to the sheer volume of its media output. The Mexico City-based companies Televisa and TV Azteca produce the bulk of the Spanish-language serialized melodramas known as *telenovelas*. Music companies like Fonovisa, as well as Mexican subsidiaries of Columbia Records and Warner Music Group, handle some of the country's most famous music exports. Mexican actors, directors, and writers are quickly becoming major players in the increasingly global entertainment industry, and, of course, there's been a steady stream of successful films that use Mexico City as a backdrop. Primarily American and European productions shot in the last 30 years, these films take advantage of the city's rich visual resources, from dense, dilapidated middle-class neighborhoods to ultra-swank hillside mansions; from well-known historical and architectural landmarks to Aztec ruins and other ephemera from long-dead civilizations.

One need not go further than the **Colonia Condesa** neighborhood to take the city's cinematic pulse. Centrally located, near the lush Parque Chapultepec, Condesa is one of the city's most ethnically and stylistically diverse neighborhoods, and about as bohemian as 21st-century Mexico City gets. Here, ultrasexy contemporary buildings mingle with vintage tiled art-deco townhouses. Nearby is a circular street that takes its shape from a previously existing equestrian club. Called **Colonia Hipodromo Condesa**, it houses a bevy of design and entertainment professionals, including architect Alberto Kalach and José Alfredo Rangel Arroyo, a.k.a. Joselo, guitarist of the popular Mexican alt-rock band Café Tacuba.

On Avenida Culiacan one finds the **Canana Films** offices. Founded by two of Mexico's most popular young actors, Diego Luna and Gael Garcia Bernal—who both starred in director Alfonso Cuarón's 2002 international hit, *Y Tu Mamá Tambien*—Canana is already one of the region's leading film finance

and distribution outfits. Along with production partner Pablo Cruz, Luna and Garcia Bernal have been steadily producing a string of critically acclaimed low-budget features like *J.C. Chavez* (2007), a documentary about a famous Mexican boxer, and *Cochochi* (2007), a drama about two boys crossing the desert, shot in Raramuri, an indigenous Northern Mexican dialect.

If Canana Film is the epicenter of independent Mexican cinema, **Estudios Churubusco** (Public tours of Churubusco Studios are $30 a person) is its reference point—the embodiment of Mexico's film heritage. Located in Colonia Coyoacan, in the city's Churubusco neighborhood, Estudios Churubusco is one of North America's most revered and longest-operating studios. Like Cincecitta in Rome and Shepperton in London, Churubusco is a tangled mass of small office buildings interspersed with hulking soundstages and warehouses. There is something about the place that is quintessentially *Mexican*. Perhaps it's the blue and adobe-colored paint applied to a series of office buildings around a small, crystalline pool. Or maybe it's the presence of tall, narrow evergreens throughout the studio lot. Whatever the visual cue, there is no doubt that Churubusco has the same color and atmosphere that one sees while strolling Chapultepec Park or canoeing on Lake Xochimilco. The place feels rooted in Mexico's history.

In a sense, it is. Churubusco was the nerve center of film production during the golden age of Mexican cinema. Founded in 1945, the studio has grown from a collection of meager stages to a network of offices and production facilities. Here was where wildly popular Mexican westerns starring early cultural exports like Antonio Aguilar and Gloria Beltran were filmed. Later, in the 1960s and '70s, Churubusco produced a bevy of films starring a younger generation of actor-singers like Pedro Infante. Their names may be unfamiliar to English-speaking audiences, but these stars embodied *ranchero* style, dressed in suede, silver-studded chaps and short coats, bright bandanas and ascots, and that ever-familiar wide-brimmed hat. Churubusco even exported its own series of comedy and action films, the most famous of which starred Mario Moreno, also known as Cantinflas, a Mexican combination of Buster Keaton and Jacques Tati who went on to appear in various American and European productions like *Around the World in 80 Days* (1956). Also popular outside Mexico during the '60s and '70s were Churubusco films featuring *luchadores*, the masked wresters that are now pop-culture icons. The most famous luchador was *El Santo*, an enigmatic, white-masked vigilante who fought crime on the streets of Mexico City.

But to say that Churubusco is firmly rooted in Mexico City's cinematic past misses the point. This is a world-class facility that has also hosted some very big-budget and contemporary Hollywood fare. Recent American films produced here include Tony Scott's *Man on Fire* (2004) and Julie Taymor's *Frida* (2002). Before that Churubusco provided facilities for David Lynch's *Dune* (1984), James Cameron's *Titanic* (1997), and Baz Luhrmann's *Romeo+Juliet* (1996). Churubusco, like Filmbyen in Denmark or Pinewood Studios in England, owes its success to the fact that it is a self-sufficient production facility. The complex not only houses various film finance and distribution outfits but offers the latest in post-production technologies. It is Mexico City's own film neighborhood.

But though Canana and Churubusco are critical locations for Mexico's film industry, the most important location of all is Mexico City itself. A host of contemporary directors like Alfonso Cuaron, Guillermo Del Toro and Alejandro Gomez Iñarritu have used the city as a backdrop for some of their most important work. In Gomez Iñarritu's groundbreaking *Amores Perros*

(2000), the action takes place in three basic locations: the dense middle-class hovels of the city's center, posh apartments near **Chapultepec Park**, and ash heaps and junkyards in the outer-ring suburbs. For *Cronos* (1993), Del Toro's first feature, the antique shops, crowded alleys, and seedy bars of the old bohemian Zona Rosa neighborhood provide a rich setting. And in *Y Tu Mama Tambien*, Cuaron's comic and sexually provocative social commentary, the action starts in the city's residential high-rises before moving to the mountain roads of Oaxaca.

These locations are not obvious. Indeed, only a local scout or someone with intimate knowledge of the city would be able to find many of them. But the cineaste or film junkie visiting the city will find that many popular tourist sites have filmic significance as well. In fact, it's possible to take a low-key tour of Mexico City's familiar sights strictly to appreciate how they have been depicted in film.

In the **Zona Central**, where one finds the greatest concentration of government buildings, is the **Plaza de la Constitución**, the city's historic center. Known as the *Zócalo*, the plaza consists of a square flanked by two buildings, the original **Basilica**, a neo-Baroque church built in the early 19th century, and the **Governmental Palace**. The latter, a popular tourist site, is a large, multistory stone building with ornate crenellations that give it the appearance of a castle. Inside is a large square, from the center of which one can observe the building's circulation patterns. Each floor has a covered walkway with ornate handrails, and along these walkways one finds one of the city's artistic treasures: a series of large **murals by Diego Rivera** depicting the history of Mexico. The triumphs and tragedies of the nation's history are presented here in Rivera's signature style. Some scenes depict the city's Aztec origins (Mexico City was once known as *Tenochtitlan*, the center of the Mesoamerican world); others show historic struggles, from civil wars to the Cristero rebellion and workers' strikes. There's something almost cinematic about Rivera's wide-format historical panoramas; as one walks from the lower to the upper walkways, the history of Mexico unspools much like a film.

Countless movies feature the **Zócalo**'s historic buildings. But to get a sense of how this part of the city fits into the urban fabric, consider one brief sequence from Steven Soderbergh's *Traffic* (2000). As Cliff Martinez's ambient soundtrack swells and drifts in the background, a small helicopter flies before it lands on the roof of a building. Aerial shots dominate the screen as the city unfurls beneath the flight path. But right before the helicopter lands, there is a shot of the Zócalo.

From the air, the building seems to tilt, an effect caused by the helicopter banking in midair. In this brief moment the square joins its larger urban context. Streets, avenues, and walkways can be seen feeding into the square. It's a privileged view that not every tourist can enjoy. But even from the ground a visit to the Zócalo leaves the impression of both historic and cinematic importance.

∧ *Traffic*, 2000. photo: ©Bedford Falls Production/Everett Collection
‹ **Zocalo** photo: ©Carlos Lozano

77

79

The same could be said of the **Chapultepec Castle**, a heavily fortified estate near Mexico City's Chapultepec Park. The building, built in an Italinate style, overlooks the evergreen forests of the park and the nearby **Zona Arqueologica**, and is firmly ingrained in Mexicans' popular imagination. The castle, which once housed a military academy for the children of Mexico's elite, was the site of a famous standoff with invading U.S. Army and Navy forces during the Mexican-American war. The academy's young pupils—the *niños heroes*, or "young heroes" of Mexican fame—defended the castle until they were killed or captured. Today Chapultepec Castle houses a history museum that details this and other moments in Mexican history.

The castle's meticulous Renaissance-style grounds stand in jarring contrast to the famous filth of the smoggy city; from here one can see both ostentatious wealth and abject poverty, serene parkland and bustling city streets. These stark contrasts lend the city a particular type of shabbiness that, much like Berlin, sparks all the senses, for better or worse. This may have been on Baz Luhrmann's mind when, for his 1996 hit *Romeo+Juliet*, he shot exteriors of the Capulet stronghold at Chapultepec Castle. But though the exterior masonry may be familiar to anyone who has visited the landmark, the interior scenes were shot at Churubusco studios.

One Mexico City location that has been mined for its interiors and exteriors, its history, and its unique ability to capture an essential "Mexican" quality is **Frida Kahlo's house**. Known as the **Casa Azul**, or Blue House, this was where Kahlo grew up and where she returned shortly before her death. Leon Trotsky also lived here for a short while when he first arrived in Mexico in 1937. To stay true to Kahlo's life, as well as to capture the unique visual qualities of her world, director Julie Taymor shot many scenes of her biopic *Frida* inside the Casa Azul.

Located on Calle Londres in Mexico City's Colonia Del Carmen Coyoacan, near the Coyoacan Viveron metro station, the Casa Azul has been a museum since 1958. Painted a brilliant cerulean blue, this jewel of a house—an adobe cottage covered in a dense tangle of plants and ironwork—makes up for its small stature with an unparalleled visual richness. Inside one can find many of the personal effects (and a small amount of artwork) of Kahlo and her husband, Diego Rivera. To get a better sense of Kahlo's creative output one must venture to other parts of the city: many of her paintings are located in Dolores Olmedo Patiño Museum in Xochimilco and the Modern Art Museum in Chapultepec Park. But Rivera's studio, designed by the modernist architect and art critic Juan O'Gorman and also featured in Taymor's film, is the place to fully appreciate the muralist's career. Conveniently, it is connected to Kahlo's house by a bridge.

These examples are only the beginning of sites that would interest the traveling film buff. The most serious and dedicated of film nerds could visit a host of other sites that have been featured, for example, in Mexican horror and science fiction films and documentaries. Fortunately, Mexico City is brimming with visual cues to its rich history, and many of them have been commemorated on celluloid. §

Enrique Ramirez is an architectural historian who writes about cities and film.

05

PICTURE PERFECT
PUERTO RICO

JOSE LUSTRE, JR.
Most memorable experience in film/travel: *Contact* inspired my curiosity about what lay beyond my backyard. The world begged discovery. I've found that hearty traveling can educate and challenge the way nothing else can.

• **Arecibo**
"El Radar" Observatory

• **San Juan**
Fort San Felipe
Old San Juan
Bahia de San Juan

Culebra

Vieques
Esperanza

The farther you drive inland in Puerto Rico, the less iguana roadkill you see. The smooth, generous lanes of the larger autopistas give way to narrow bands of concrete in various phases of disrepair. Two-lane roads undulate between hills and limestone formations. Fields turn into jungles. This is the road to El Radar.

The **Arecibo Observatory**, or "El Radar" to the locals, is the largest radio telescope in the world. The dish spans 1,000 feet across and covers an area roughly equivalent to 26 football fields. The complex is enclosed by thick jungle and the dish itself is cradled inside a natural sinkhole. The telescope examines our atmosphere from just a few miles above sea level. But it can detect signals from as far as 10 billion light years away.

Arecibo's enormity, scientific importance, and curious surroundings attracted filmmakers not long after scientists from all over the world began to book time at the observatory. An episode of the *X-Files* was filmed here. So too were climactic scenes from the James Bond movie *GoldenEye* (1995), where the observatory stood in for a top-secret satellite dish in Cuba. But its more

accurate portrayal in the 1997 film *Contact*, in which Jodie Foster plays an astronomer whose interest in extraterrestrial civilizations leads her to Arecibo, gave the site unprecedented attention. In the film Arecibo is depicted as the ideal facility for Foster to conduct her survey of interstellar life. But somebody pulls the plug. At a climactic moment Foster drives a 4x4 up the rough road to the observatory to confront the man who cut funding for her research.

But if a deep-space search for aliens is being conducted at El Radar, most of it remains hidden to the 100,000 visitors Arecibo sees each year. Instead, a museum situated near the rim of the dish shares the history of

⌃ *Contact,* 1997. photo: ©Everett Collection
‹ **Arecibo Observatory** photo: ©Tex Photo
[previous page] **Old San Juan, Puerto Rico** photo: ©Sasha Burt

the observatory and explains—in layman's terms—the science behind radio astronomy. A theater shows a short film on the daily operations of the observatory and follows a guest scientist on a typical day.

A visit to Arecibo culminates in viewing the dish from the observatory. The real thing is not like what is shown in the movies. Its size is astonishing, but the surface of the dish does not glimmer under the sun. In fact the composite tiles are dingy and a close look reveals an entire ecosystem thriving in the underbrush. This is technology in the midst of flora and fauna; man's technological march alongside the inexorable progress of nature. As it scans the ionosphere and outer heavens, Arecibo also functions as a fitting symbol of Puerto Rico's history of intersecting forces, of the disparate influences that have converged on this tiny island and tried to move forward in unison.

Even before the U.S. invaded the island during the Spanish-American War, Puerto Rico's history was already characterized by overlapping cultures and military takeovers. Tainos and Caribs were the first inhabitants of the island. Then came the Spaniards, and the Portuguese and the Dutch. African slaves were introduced to the island and the British lodged attacks against it. For centuries, resilient Puerto Rico has absorbed foreign cultural and military powers. Nowhere on the island is this more evident than in the capital city of **San Juan**.

At the northwest corner of San Juan is **Fort San Felipe del Morro**, simply known as **El Morro**. Thanks to its massive size and its historical importance— it's purported to be the oldest Spanish fort in the Americas and became a UNESCO World Heritage site in 1983—this citadel sees more than two million visitors each year. Steven Spielberg transformed El Morro into a West African slave fortress in the 1997 film *Amistad*. At the end of the movie, the British Royal Navy bombards the fort and liberates imprisoned slaves.

In real life El Morro was constructed in the mid-1500s by the Spaniards. The fort successfully fended off British and Dutch attacks, but centuries later, during the Spanish-American War, the U.S. Navy proved too overwhelming. Six months after hostilities commenced, Puerto Rico was handed over to the United States. American military forces manned the fort during both world wars but abandoned the complex in 1961.

The grounds were later converted into baseball fields, medical facilities, and a golf course. What was once the Field of Fire—450 yards of completely open space designed to expose any intruders who managed to penetrate the walls—now beckons soccer players and joggers. Children play and explore around the ramparts and embankments. At the tip of El Morro, a lighthouse continues to guide passing vessels. (The original lighthouse was destroyed by American forces. It was rebuilt in 1899 and over the last few decades has been the focal point of El Morro.)

A short walk inland from the fort leads tourists to the heart of Puerto Rico, **Old San Juan**. Like El Morro, Old San Juan's history is palpable. As the city adapts to suit the increasingly sophisticated mix of visitors, the cobblestone streets and plazas are staunch guardians of its past. The narrow roads that were once an easily navigable grid for pedestrians are now crowded with luxury cars. Lights from restaurants reflect in the stone steps of old churches and plazas. Hip-hop and reggaeton pulse in Old San Juan's humid air. But an unintended turn or the loss of a map can reveal another side of Old San Juan.

Narrow two-story residences are often just a block away from the crowded plazas. With a style characterized by pastel hues, white accents, arches

 and wrought-iron gates, these homes have retained much of the charm associated with Spanish colonial architecture. This aesthetic was prevalent in many islands in the Caribbean, and parts of *Dirty Dancing 2: Havana Nights* and *Bad Boys II* were filmed here because of the city's resemblance to Havana. Because of its strained relations with the west, and especially with the United States, Cuba cannot play itself on film; many of its stories have been told by proxy in San Juan.

Puerto Rico's own domestic cinema has been overshadowed by foreign productions on the island. Famed director Jacobo Morales received the country's sole Academy Award nomination for Best Foreign Language

film for *Lo que pasó a Santiago* (1990). But Puerto Rican talent continues to make an impact worldwide. Actors Benicio Del Toro, Rita Moreno, and José Ferrer have all won Oscars; Moreno, in fact, is one of a handful of entertainers to have won an Oscar, Tony, Emmy, and Grammy award.

Most who visit Puerto Rico are looking for the postcard-worthy beach: Soft white sand, gentle breezes and crystalline water in various shades of blue.

Those beaches can be found on the island of **Vieques**, just off the coast. Along with **Culebra**, its smaller sister island, Vieques is an ideal alternative for travelers who are willing to sacrifice the comforts of St. Barts or St. Martin. It is less developed than Jamaica and offers many secluded beaches. But as with many parts of Puerto Rico, military forces have had a hand in shaping its history.

Twenty-one miles across and five miles wide, Vieques is the larger of the two Spanish Virgin Islands. At the close of the 20th century, after 100 years of military presence, protestors from Puerto Rico and other nations demanded the expulsion of the U.S. Navy from the island. The protests came to a head in 1999 when a bombing exercise went awry and left one civilian dead. In May of 2003 the navy left the island for good and ceded much of Vieques back to its citizens. Locals and expats continue to learn how to harness the natural beauty of the island, 70 percent of which was, ironically, preserved within the military bases. Vieques has so far avoided what many predict is an inevitable influx of international developers and their resort ambitions. The tourism industry is in its infancy, but world-class restaurants forecast a future that may soon challenge the unspoiled splendor of the island.

Esperanza is on the southern coast of the island and acts as the launching point from where visitors can explore its many beaches. The small town's main road borders the ocean and features many restaurants and hotels. There are few locals here and the high price of accommodations and meals attracts an even more select subgroup of the foreigners who come to Puerto

∧ *Dirty Dancing: Havana Nights*, 2004. photo: ©Miramax/Everett Collection
‹ **Vieques** photo: ©dmotif [next page] **Vieques Coastline** photo: ©Victor Nieves

Rico. Nearby markets offer cheap alternatives, but fresh catches of the day are served by some of Puerto Rico's best chefs and are worth the splurge.

While many rent vehicles to reach the beaches, a group of nearby options is within walking distance. **Sun Bay,** directly east of Esperanza, has a large crescent shoreline. Because it is also accessible by car—there is a large parking lot—and allows camping, this beach can be more crowded than adjacent alternatives. Sun Bay is also home to wild horses, which are often seen grazing in the area. Farther east, down a rough dirt road is **Playa Media Luna**, a smaller and more tranquil spot that attracts many visiting Puerto Rican families. There are few amenities here, just a few trashcans and picnic tables. The next beach to the east, **Playa Navio**, is even more secluded, but is the most beautiful of the three. Early beachgoers are often rewarded by having this beach all to themselves for hours.

The untouched coves and beaches inspired Peter Brook to choose Vieques as the location for his 1963 adaptation of William Golding's classic novel

Lord of the Flies, the tale of a group of small boys who, after a plane crash kills all adult passengers, must learn to cope with a strange environment. Sun Bay is shown throughout the beginning of the movie, as the boys survey their new surroundings, begin to build shelters and learn to keep a signal fire lit. As their society develops, the group splits in two, with one group devoted to hunting wild boar. But this division spirals into tribal warfare as the hunters—who discover in Media Luna how to smoke an indigenous plant— become increasingly violent and even murderous.

Though they served as the backdrop for some of the film's more savage scenes, these beaches now offer the pristine and relaxed atmosphere that many who come to Puerto Rico are searching for. For many, however, it is **Bahia Mosquito**—just east of Media Luna—that leaves the most lasting impression.

Bahia Mosquito is one of the best bioluminescent bays on earth. The water is home to dinoflagellates, which are fed by the mangrove trees. These small creatures have a unique way of communicating danger. When they sense a predator, the dinoflagellates light up. When I visited it was fairly late at night, and my small group of tourists slid into kayaks and paddled quietly away from the shore, avoiding the wild mangrove branches that covered the shores of the lagoon.

As our paddles cut into the surface of the water, a faint trail of iridescent bubbles seemed to be left behind. The farther we went, the brighter the lights. The enclosed nature of the bay is responsible not only for the temperature of the water but also for the bioluminescent phenomenon. The mangrove's nutrients are protected from open seas and allow the glowing creatures to thrive.

After paddling for 15 minutes, we tied our kayaks together, forming a floating island, and jumped into the water. My entire body lit up. Each movement of an arm, a leg, was matched by an eerie glow. I was covered in illuminated crystals and left struggling for an explanation.

Though the military in Vieques has formally left, vestiges of their presence linger. Abandoned military structures are being converted to civilian use. Conversations with local residents often reveal stories about the navy's role in the island and the hole it left behind. Before swimming back to the kayaks I floated on my back for a minute. Less than a decade ago it would not have been unusual to hear the explosion of bombs from this very location in Bahia Mosquito. I began to swing my arms, each stroke accompanied by nature's most beautiful call to arms. §

Jose Lustre Jr. saw *Apocalypse Now* as a 14-year-old and immediately planned a visit to Saigon. He made good on his promise and has since outrun a rock avalanche in the Himalayas, been hit by a truck in Indonesia and people-watched in downtown Ramallah. He recovers in Los Angeles, where he is a writer and an IT manager. He holds a degree in Print Journalism and Film Production from the University of Southern California.

‹ **Culebra Military Base** photo: ©David Sanchez
[next page] **Moraine Lake** photo: ©Mike Norton

06

IDEAS
OF NORTH
CANADA

JASON ANDERSON
Most memorable experience in film/travel: Playing hooky at Sundance by having a glorious day of skiing at Deer Valley that unfortunately had to be cut short for a *Little Miss Sunshine* screening. And enjoying the enormous fresh shellfish platters at Chez Astoux in Cannes, which made the festival grind a lot easier to bear.

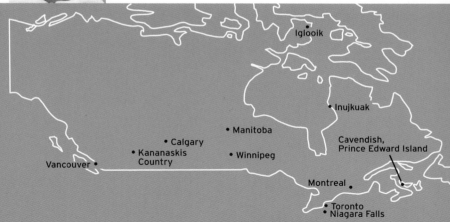

Iglooik

Inujkuak

Calgary
Kananaskis
Country

Manitoba

Winnipeg

Cavendish,
Prince Edward Island

Vancouver

Montreal

Toronto
Niagara Falls

"Canada," Marshall McLuhan once wrote,

"is the only country in the world that knows how to live without an identity." The residents of this corner of what the late University of Toronto professor dubbed the global village may bristle at the unkillable notion of Canada as a place without a face. Yet they are also leery of the icons that have long represented the country internationally, be they beavers, Mounties or red-haired lassies from Green Gables. When asked to choose between hazy blandness and maple-flavored kitsch, we mostly do the Canadian thing and politely pretend we didn't hear the question. Cinematic portrayals of Canadian places are often informed by the same ambiguity and ambivalence. Though the world's second largest country, it can often seem like its biggest movie set—especially given how often Hollywood has come north to make use of the scenery, and how rarely it admits where these majestic vistas are actually located.

It's a strange but common feeling for audiences in the urban centers of Toronto, Montreal and Vancouver to sit in a multiplex and see landmarks that are literally within meters of where they happen to be while the characters onscreen insist they're in Washington or New York. That fourth-wall-busting predicament was especially pronounced for Toronto viewers during the finale of *The Incredible Hulk* (2008), where **Yonge Street**'s downtown main drag was relocated to Harlem, if solely through the digital superimposition of the Apollo Theater's marquee and a hair braiding salon alongside such familiar establishments as **The Big Slice** pizza shop and the gentleman's club known as the **Zanzibar Tavern**. (You can see the club's actual interior when Jean-Claude Van Damme dashes through it in 1996's *Maximum Risk*.)

Though the country's natural splendor and malleable streetscapes have been endlessly deployed in service of foreign productions, making movies in Canada doesn't always come down to the Yankee dollar. (Or the Euro for that matter—though the German tax-shelter productions of much-parodied director Uwe Boll have poured over $100 million into the B.C. film industry in recent years.) Since the Canadian scene came of age in the late

< **Yonge Street, Toronto** photo: ©SNEHIT

60s, filmmakers have doggedly tried to capture stories and sights from every corner of the country. Whether these efforts collectively constitute what McLuhan would consider a coherent "identity" is up for debate, but directors like David Cronenberg, Bruce Sweeney and Deepa Mehta have chosen to emphasize the particularity of their locations rather than disguise them.

With that in mind, we provide a cross-Canada tour through sites of cinematic significance, some of which actually get to keep their real names.

WESTWARD HO

While our neighbors to the south gobbled up the western frontier, Canadians were laxer about filling every available square foot of real estate with Wal-Marts. As a result, the Canadian west has become a favorite substitute for the long-gone American incarnation. Such westerns as *Unforgiven* (1992), *Legends of the Fall* (1994), *Open Range* (2003) and *The Assassination of Jesse James by the Coward Robert Ford* (2007) were all filmed largely in southern Alberta, especially in the areas outside Calgary where the rolling foothills and wide-open prairie butt up against the

Rocky Mountains. But these landscapes were arguably best displayed in *Brokeback Mountain* (2005), which might be set in Wyoming but could still serve as a promotional ad for the area known as **Kananaskis Country**. Visitors inclined to restage the cowboys' romance for themselves can head out to sites at **Moose Mountain**, **Goat Creek**, **Elbow Falls** and **Upper Kananaskis Lake**—even the old church in the town of Dinton where Heath Ledger's character pledges to stay true to the precepts of heterosexuality. Unfortunately, you can no longer visit the frontier town of Presbyterian Church, which was originally built in West Vancouver for the purposes of another great western, Robert Altman's *McCabe & Mrs. Miller* (1971). One of the earliest major features to be shot in British Columbia, it anticipated the Hollywood gold rush precipitated by the weak Canadian dollar in the late 80s and 90s.

∧ *Brokeback Mountain,* 2005. photo: ©Focus Features/Everett Collection
‹ **Kananaskis Lake** photo: ©B.G. Smith [next page] **Niagara Falls** photo: ©BlueSoul Photography

VAN CITY

Though the Vancouver area took all comers once the movie bucks started flowing in, it developed a special forte for geek-pleasing TV shows—*The X-Files, Battlestar Galactica, Supernatural, Smallville*—and unnecessary movie sequels—*Scooby Doo 2: Monsters Unleashed* (2004), *Final Destination 3* (2006), *Fantastic Four: Rise of the Silver Surfer* (2007). The city's architectural landmarks inevitably came into heavy use, especially the **Vancouver Public Library** (done up to look extrafuturistic in 2000's Schwarzenegger actioner *The Sixth Day* and the **Marine Building**. The latter, an art deco wonder on Burrard Street, was seen in both *Fantastic Four* movies, and serves as the Daily Planet headquarters on *Smallville*.

Downtown Vancouver's classic northern-city urbanity and cleanliness, while attractive to foreign producers and location scouts, have led its own directors to emphasize its grittier and less inviting side, be it the drab working-class housing in Larry Kent's *The Bitter Ash* (1963), the bleak, drug-ridden Downtown East Side dives in Nathaniel Geary's *On the Corner* (2003) or the notoriously shoddy "leaky condos" that the characters in Bruce Sweeney's *Last Wedding* (2001) call home.

Retreat into the province's mountainous interior and matters get more picturesque. The quaintly pretty town of **Nelson, B.C.** was where Steve Martin famously wooed Daryl Hannah (by proxy due to his oversized proboscis) in *Roxanne* (1987). Over the border in Alberta, the majestic **Fairmont Banff Springs Hotel** once played host to Marilyn Monroe, in *River of No Return* (1954), directed by Otto Preminger. Confusingly, the Raoul Walsh thriller *Saskatchewan* (1954) was also shot in the Banff area, rather than the eponymous province. For a fix of authentic swathes of Saskatchewan plain, try Terry Gilliam's *Tideland* (2005)—fields of wheat never looked weirder.

CITIES ON THE PLAIN

The oil boom has returned Calgary to the ranks of the country's wealthiest cities. But its modernity has also been better captured in homegrown efforts than less memorable Hollywood fare like *Superman 3* (1983)—though locals were happy to see the **Calgary Tower** as part of Metropolis' skyline. As you might've guessed from the title, Gary Burns' *The Suburbanators* (1995) stars a pair of slackers who take a meandering course through some of the city's most nondescript neighborhoods. The city's core—where buildings

> **Marine Building, Vancouver** photo: ©Colin Rose

like those of the **Bankers Hall** complex are connected by a system of **"Plus-15" walkways** that keep workers warm—was the appropriately banal site for Burns' satirical comedy *waydowntown* (2000). And if you want to feel like you're in *FUBAR* (2002), spend a weekend night loitering near any suburban bus shelter.

Winnipeg's defining economic boom, however, came and went long ago. As a result, its many well-preserved historical buildings have become a popular location for Hollywood period dramas. A 30-block showcase of turn-of-the-century architecture, the **Exchange District** became 1950s New York for *Capote* (2005) and various 60s locations in *Across the Universe* (2007). Yet the city received its sincerest love letter when hometown boy **Guy Maddin** made *My Winnipeg* (2007), a docu-fantasy intermingling Maddin's family history with frequently dubious facts about the hometown he loves and loathes. Did city elders really invite prostitutes to séances held in the **Manitoba Legislative Building**? The Masonic details in the design suggest something was up when the building was completed in 1920.

THE R.C. HARRIS WATER TREATMENT PLANT

For a building that has given so many decades of honorable service to Torontonians, the R.C. Harris Water Treatment Plant (also referred to as the R.C. Harris Filtration Plant) has a rather fearsome reputation. One of the city's most distinctive film locations, it has served as the setting for prisons, asylums and, yes, the headquarters of many shadowy, SPECTRE-like outfits.

Of course, this was never the building's intended purpose. Located at the foot of Victoria Park Avenue, the plant resides on the eastern edge of Toronto's shoreline in the neighborhood known as the Beaches (though many residents will be more than happy to tell you that the Beach is the proper historical name). Details of the plant's construction and that of the Prince Edward Viaduct (which spans the Don Valley between Bloor Street and Danforth Avenue) figure prominently in what may be the best novel ever written about the city: *In the Skin of a Lion*, by Michael Ondaatje. (Moviegoers may be better acquainted with that book's sequel, *The English Patient*.)

In the building's design, architect Thomas C. Pomphrey would integrate elements of the beaux arts style (an architectural school more strongly represented locally by Union Station, finished in 1927) as well as art deco. So while its purpose may be sensibly utilitarian, the plant is also undeniably grand. Given its cathedral-like façade and marble entryways, it's no wonder the place was once dubbed "a palace of purification."

Yet it often doubles as the perfect place from which to take over the world. In the comedy *Undercover Brother* (2002), it can be seen as the headquarters of the ever-oppressive forces of "The Man." On the TV shows *The Pretender* and *Mutant X*, it is the base of operations for various nefarious villains.

It's also a popular choice for penitentiaries—the plant gets serious jail time in the action thriller *The Long Kiss Goodnight* (1996) and the stoner comedy *Half Baked* (1998). Other location scouts apparently believe the gothic touch added by those cathedral-like details makes it more appropriate as a home for the criminally insane. Such was its fate in *RoboCop: The Series* and John Carpenter's *In the Mouth of Madness* (1992).

Yet of all of the movies and TV shows that have presented the R.C. Harris Water Treatment Plant as a place where bad things happen, one has strongly sentimental value to Canadians. In *Strange Brew* (1983)—the sole big-screen outing for Bob and Doug McKenzie, the much-loved hosers played by Rick Moranis and Dave Thomas on the comedy series *SCTV*—the plant can be seen in the guise of the Elsinore Brewery. Much as so many filmmakers have cast a sinister light on this otherwise noble provider of clean drinking water for thirsty Torontonians, the movie's lead villain (played by Max Von Sydow) perverts the fictional brewery's fundamental purpose as the purveyor of sudsy goodness with his evil schemes for world domination. Now that's a real crime.

MONTREAL, JE T'AIME

Until the French separatist movement of the 60s and 70s drove the Anglo money into Toronto, Montreal was Canada's favorite city. It remains well loved by citizens, tourists and filmmakers alike. The vintage European look of the **Old Port** has made it especially handy as a substitute for old-world locales such as 1920s Paris in Alan Rudolph's *The Moderns* (1988). At the same time, this is also the city where such FX spectaculars as *300* (2007), *The Day After Tomorrow* (2004) and *The Fountain* (2007) were made. Indeed, Hollywood enjoys Montreal so much one of its recent productions actually went so far as to acknowledge the city by name. In *The Score* (2001), thieves played by Robert De Niro, Edward Norton and Marlon Brando are out to pinch a 17th-century French scepter being stored at the **Customs House** in Old Montreal, originally built in 1836 as Britain's first major architectural contribution to the New World. De Niro's character even runs a jazz club in Montreal called "NYC" for cover—a nice bit of irony given how many times the city has played the Big Apple.

But Quebec's most renowned director, Denys Arcand, made the quintessential Montreal film.

> **Old Port, Montreal** photo: ©Action Photos
[next page] **CN Tower, Toronto** photo: ©Elena Elisseeva

The city is vividly captured in his *Jesus of Montreal* (1989), a drama about a group of actors who put a very modern spin on the Passion play, which takes place at a shrine up on **Mont Royal**. When the young man playing the Messiah (Lothaire Bluteau) takes the role too far, he suffers a climactic collapse in the **Place-St-Henri** metro station, transforming this most functional of urban spaces into a site of high drama.

TORONTO STORIES

When the stars aren't making their annual trip down the red carpet for glitzy premieres during the Toronto International Film Festival every September, they're spending their time here on movie shoots. Though the local industry was hurt badly by the SARS outbreak in 2003 and the loonie's mid-decade rise against the American dollar, it remains a favorite for Hollywood—such hits as *X-Men* (2000), *Hairspray* (2007) and *The Incredible Hulk* (2008) were all filmed in Toronto. A real chameleon, the city has doubled for Detroit in *Four Brothers* (2005) and *Assault on Precinct 13* (2005), New York in *16 Blocks* (2006) and *Jumper* (2007) and Chicago in *John Q* (2002), *My Big Fat Greek Wedding* (2002) and yes, even *Chicago* (2002). Though filmmakers usually avoid the sight of the city's most recognizable landmark—the **CN Tower**, the world's tallest freestanding structure until it was surpassed by the Burj Dubai in 2007—it inevitably pops up from time to time. It even costarred with Jennifer Lopez in *Angel Eyes* (2001), hampering the movie's claim that it too was set in Chicago.

Certain locations are more freely used—the curved towers and large public plaza of **City Hall** can be seen in relatively contemporary form in *The Sentinel* (2007) and in more futuristic guise in *Resident Evil: Apocalypse* (2004). Opened in 1927 and built in the beaux arts style, **Union Station** stars in *Cinderella Man* (2005) and *Mr. Magorium's Wonder Emporium* (2007)—a train even busts through one of its walls in *Silver Streak* (1976). A faux-English castle whose construction costs eventually ruined owner Sir Henry Mill Pellatt in the 1930s, **Casa Loma**'s dignified interiors and exteriors were put to use in *X-Men* (2000), *The Pacifier* (2005) and *The Love Guru* (2008).

⌃ **Cinderella Man**, 2005. photo: ©Universal/Everett Collection
‹ **Union Station, Toronto** photo: ©Alex Tsiboulski

By now, Toronto's citizens are so used to the sight of trailers and orange parking pylons it takes a lot for them to get excited about a shoot. At times, the city's propensity for disguises can be downright disorienting. Walking near Queen's Park early one Sunday morning years ago, I was surprised to discover that Toronto had its own Watergate Hotel—alas, the sign was only part of a neighborhood makeover for the Washington-set comedy *Dick* (1999). No wonder we're confused when the city is allowed to play itself.

A former "baron of blood" who's gone on to become Toronto's most celebrated filmmaker, David Cronenberg typically shoots his movies here, his austere aesthetic accentuated by the chilly modern look of spaces like the Scarborough campus of the **University of Toronto** in *Stereo* (1969) and *Crimes of the Future* (1970) and the tangle of on-ramps and flyovers on the **Gardiner Expressway** in *Crash* (1996). A warmer view of the city can be found in Deepa Mehta's *Bollywood/Hollywood* (2002), a celebration of the unique intermingling of cultures in Toronto whose production numbers are staged in such sites as the **Little India** neighborhood in the city's East End and a condominium overlooking Toronto's harbor. For an earlier view of Toronto, Don Shebib's *Goin' Down the Road* (1970) offers an indelible portrait of the city in the late 60s. The views of the pre-*Hulk* Yonge Street drag are spellbinding, especially when the lead characters make a trip to **Sam the Record Man**, the landmark music store whose giant, spinning neon sign was illuminated for the last time in 2008.

HINTERLAND WHO'S WHO

Located out on Canada's Atlantic seaboard, the Maritimes can feel like a whole other country. Movies set in Newfoundland, like *The Shipping News* (2001), emphasize its remoteness and rough weather, though small-town stories like *The Bay Boy* (1984)—featuring Kiefer Sutherland in his first major role—and *The Rowdyman* (1972) offer gentler views of life on the East Coast. Indeed, the worldwide popularity of Lucy Maud Montgomery's

---

^ *The Shipping News,* 2001. photo: ©Miramax/Everett Collection
> **Lighthouse, Prince Edward Island** photo: ©V.J. Matthew

Anne of Green Gables books (and ensuing TV series) has fostered an idyllic image of the region. Tourists flock to the fictional Anne's real-life home of Cavendish on **Prince Edward Island**. A much snarkier story of girlhood— which can be seen as a riposte to the Anne myth—is the well-loved cult movie *New Waterford Girl* (1999), whose feisty young heroine finds herself in the far dowdier context of a rough fishing port located north of Sydney.

Areas much deeper into Canada's north may attract fewer visitors, but they've also made a big impression on screen. Shot in 1920 and 1921 near **Inukjuak** on Hudson Bay, *Nanook of the North* (1922) was a pioneering documentary film by Robert J. Flaherty. A worldwide hit, it also cemented stereotypes about the Inuit among folks to the south. Decades later, a collective of Inuit filmmakers would create their own corrective to *Nanook* with *Atanarjuat: The Fast Runner* (2002), a stunning achievement widely regarded as one of the best films ever made in Canada. Hardy cine-tourists who don't see walking tours of Old Montreal or Winnipeg's Exchange District as much of a challenge can find the same Arctic landscapes they see on screen by heading up to **Iglooik**. Others may want to do like the majority of Canadians do and stay further away from the polar bears. §

Jason Anderson writes about film for such publications as *Cinema Scope*, *Toronto's Eye Weekly*, *The Globe and Mail* and *Artforum.com*. In the process, he has covered festivals in Cannes, Toronto, Vancouver and Park City, Utah. He also teaches film criticism at the University of Toronto.

07

NEW ARGENTINE CINEMA

ARGENTINA

ANDREA CHIGNOLI
Most memorable experience in film/travel: Watching a Bollywood movie in a New Delhi theater was an amazing experience that made me think there is no separation between life and film: the audience was talking and eating and smoking during the entire screening!

- Salta
- Misiones Province
- Buenos Aires [Balvanera]
- Santa Cruz
- Rio Turbio

Many readers will no doubt hear "Argentina"
and think immediately of Madonna crooning "Don't Cry for Me,
Argentina," in *Evita* (1996). The scene happens to be the only
one filmed on location in Buenos Aires; the star was morally
opposed to spending too much time in the country that loved
her titular character. But in a way, the reference is appropriate,
in that the life arc of New Argentine Cinema follows closely on
the heels of a broken down (if romanticized) dictatorship.

Culturally speaking, other readers may hear "Argentina" and think "tango,"
or of Manuel Puig, who most famously wrote *Kiss of the Spider Woman*. A
few others will hopefully think of *Happy Together* by Wong Karwai (1997),

which was actually
made on a lark after
the director found
himself "stuck" in
Buenos Aires with an
entire film production
crew that was meant
to film an axed-at-the-
last-minute adaptation
of another Puig novel.
To move away from the hyperbole of the international icons, and for the
most enriching perspective on the various landscapes that make up this
very diverse country, the work of native filmmakers is more than worth
a look.

"You know, I met a girl that used to get horny with the **Obelisco**," says
Pablo, one of the main characters in Adrián Caetano and Bruno Stagnaro's
Pizza, birra, faso ("Pizza, Beer, Smokes," 1997). "She thought the Obelisco
was a gigantic penis attracting the erotic energies of the city." This scene—
in which Pablo and a friend hang out eating pizza on a street corner in
downtown Buenos Aires—and its irreverent depiction of the city's iconic
monument in Palaza de la Republica, stuck in the memory of its Argentine
audience. The film was the spark that ignited what is now called the "New
Argentine Cinema."

^ *Happy Together,* 1997. photo: ©Block 2 Pictures/Everett Collection
< **Buenos Aires, Argentina** photo: ©Celso Diniz

Though many consider Martín Rejtman, whose cult film *Rapado* (1991) tracked a disoriented young character in his meaningless bike rides through the dull middleclass neighborhood of **Flores**, the father of this movement, the first film to collect international awards, receive positive reviews, and actually draw people to the theater was *Pizza, birra, faso*. Following a gang of street kids who wander around **Avenida Corrientes**, surviving through petty robbery, the film is a crude but realistic portrait of a city crushed by the weight of an enormous national debt—a city of 13 million in which unemployment, especially among young adults, had reached an unprecedented high. Premiering at the International Mar del Plata Film Festival in 1997, it generated more enthusiasm than any Argentine film since Luis Puenzo's *La historia oficial* ("The Official Story") won the Oscar for Best Foreign Film in 1986.

At the time *La historia oficial* was released, Argentina was recovering from almost a decade of dictators that resulted in nearly 30,000 *desaparecidos* ("disappeared") and a failed war against the British in the Falkland Islands. The eagerly awaited return of democracy meant, among other things, the rebuilding of a national cinema that had been until then harshly censored.

La historia oficial depicts the search of a history professor who comes to realize that her adopted daughter is the child of a *desaparecido*. That realization is also a spatial journey, covering symbolic sites within Buenos Aires. At the beginning of the film the main character, Alicia, meets her conservative friends, all of them supporters of the military, in the fancy **Cáfe Richmond**, at 468 Florida Street. Later, she witnesses an enormous demonstration led by the so-called Mothers of the Plaza de Mayo, which takes place in the actual **Plaza de Mayo**, the main square around which the city was built. Through the years of corrupt military dictatorships the Mothers of the Plaza de Mayo congregated there with signs and pictures of *desaparecidos*, taking advantage of the central location to raise public consciousness about the military's actions.

A great number of the films that followed *La historia oficial* had a similar goal: to reveal the brutality of the "Dirty War," which lasted from 1976 to 1983. Hector Olivera's *La noche de los lápices* ("The Night of the Pencils," 1986) narrated the horror of the kidnapping, forced disappearances and torture of a number of high school students. Bebe Kamin's *Los chicos de la guerra* ("Boys

---

Mothers of the Plaza de Mayo Demonstration photo: ©Matias Miranda
[next page] **Buenos Aires National Congress** photo: ©Eduardo Rivero

of War," 1986) dealt with the failure of the Falklands War and its effect on three young conscripts. Pino Solanas's *Sur* ("The South," 1988) described the difficulties faced by a former exile on his return to his old neighborhood in Buenos Aires.

This last contains an emblematic sequence in which the famous singer Roberto Goyeneche sings a tango at the most cinematic corner of Buenos Aires, just one block from the old Hipólito Yrigoyen train station and the just-renovated tango bar **El Barracas**, which has been the location of several features, including Leonardo Favio's *Gatica, el mono* (1993) and the American production *Naked Tango*, by Leonard Schrader (1991). This over-sentimental sequence in *Sur* summarizes the nostalgia for sensual bohemian life that the protagonist can't find anymore in the new, depressed city. But it also reflects the ways which Argentine cinema had become artificial, mannered, and clichéd.

By 1997 a new generation of moviemakers was facing a new set of challenges. The New Argentine Cinema directors shared the social concerns of their predecessors, but they developed an unaffected aesthetic that broke with the old, marked by a loose camera, the regular use of nonprofessional actors, and naturalistic dialogue heavy on slang. In combination these elements produce an extremely realistic result; some of the films straddle the boundary between documentary and fiction.

The film world took notice. *Mundo grúa* ("Crane World," 2001), Pablo Trapero's first feature, won the FIPRESCI Prize and the Tiger Award at the Rotterdam Film Festival. *Bolivia*, Adrián Caetano's followup to *Pizza, birra, faso*, was acclaimed at Cannes in 2001, the same year that Lucrecia Martel's *La ciénaga* ("The Swamp") won the Alfred Bauer Award at the Berlin Film Festival.

One of the innovations of Martel's films, apart from her inspired camerawork and delicate sound design, is the location she chose for her three features, which include, in addition to *La ciénaga, La niña santa* ("The Holy Girl," 2004) and *La mujer sin cabeza* ("The Headless Woman," 2008). She shot in her hometown of **Salta**, a city in northwestern Argentina, the capital city of the Salta Province and now a major tourist destination thanks to its colonial architecture and the natural beauty of

> **Salta, Argentina** photo: ©jorisvo

the valleys to the west. Martel's films depict both the lovely landscape of the rainforest-clad hills and the racial heterogeneity of the city, which is also inhabited by indigenous Aymara communities. One of the most violent scenes in *La ciénaga*, in which a main character gets into a bloody fight after getting drunk at a local Aymara festival, illustrated the racial tensions of the region.

After the success of his *El bonaerense* (2002), Pablo Trapero took Martel's search for natural beauty as an example and made his fourth film as a road movie. *Familia rodante* ("Rolling Family," 2004) tells the story of a dysfunctional working-class family on a trip from Buenos Aires to **Yapeyú, Corrientes**, in the northeast of the country. Both family secrets and the subtropical geography of Corrientes, with its *gauchos* and its *ñandús*, are illuminated through the window of their noisy motor home.

In his fifth film, *Nacido y criado* ("Born and Bred," 2006), Trapero stayed outside Buenos Aires once more, shooting in **Río Turbio, Patagonia**. Here, the remote location mirrors the protagonist's isolation. An interior designer whose successful life is devastated in an accident seeks refuge from his grief in this bleak terrain of persistent snow and muddy roads.

Trapero is not the first director to take advantage of the rugged Patagonian landscape. Director Carlos Sorin shot two of his recent films, *Historias*

mínimas ("Intimate Stories," 2002) and *El perro* ("Bombón, the Dog," 2004), in **Santa Cruz**, another Patagonian province. In both films Sorin uses the endless road over the vast steppes of Southern Patagonia as a major character. He also relied heavily on local talent: all but two of the cast members are non-professionals who play their roles with apparently effortless naturalism.

^ *El Camino de San Diego,* 2006. photo: ©20th Century Fox de Argentina/Everett Collection
‹ **Mount Fitz Roy, Los Glaciares Patagonia, Argentina** photo: ©jorisvo
[next page] **Neuquen** photo: ©Pablo A. Puente

Hunting the most inaccessible provinces for freshness, Sorin shot his last film, *El camino de San Diego* ("The Road to San Diego," 2006), on the opposite side of Patagonia, in **Misiones Province**. A smart take on celebrity worship, the film follows the journey of Tati, a logger on the forgotten northern edge of Argentina who is convinced that he has the power to heal his football idol, a victim of drug and alcohol addictions who is hospitalized in Buenos Aires. Luis Puenzo's daughter, Lucía, another brilliant filmmaker of this new wave, explored the Atlantic seaside in her queer cinema masterpiece *XXY*, awarded the Critics Week Grand Prize at the 2007 Cannes Film Festival. Puenzo's film is the dramatic story of an intersex teenager whose well-meaning but frightened parents hide her from the world in the coastal town of **Piriápolis**. This Uruguayan summer resort, with its opulent hotels, large casinos and active nightlife, becomes an asphyxiating dungeon for the protagonist on a quest for sexual identity.

Glue: A Teenage Story in the Middle of Nowhere, written and directed by Alexis dos Santos, is another Argentine queer film that takes place in a remote area. Shot in **Neuquén**, Patagonia, in an improvisational style, this coming-of-age fable captures the wild beauty of Patagonia's windswept summer landscape. Screened at the 2007 New Directors/New Films Festival in New York City, the film also won the Best First Feature Prize at the San Francisco International Gay and Lesbian Film Festival.

But not every New Argentine filmmaker seeks inspiration in the natural landscape; some still prefer Buenos Aires. Take, for example, prizewinning director Lisandro Alonso and his silent homage to **Centro Cultural San Martín**, *Fantasma* (2006). In this peculiar film, Alonso places the characters of his previous two films in the main cultural center of the city. Misael and Argentino Vargas, the two remarkable performers who gave life to *La libertad* (2001) and *Los muertos* (2004), respectively, walk quietly around the different rooms of the cultural center like hunting ghosts that can't find

peace. In a hyperrealist conclusion the two characters encounter each other in the main screening room, where *Los muertos* is being projected.

The Jewish neighborhood of **Balvanera** (also called **Barrio Once**) is masterfully described in Daniel Burman's second feature, *El abrazo partido* ("The Lost Embrace," 2004), which won the Berlin Film Festival Jury Grand Prix. The neighborhood, the hub of the garment trade, sets the scene for the inner conflicts of Ariel Menaker (played by Uruguayan actor Daniel Hendler, who took home the Best Actor prize at Berlin), a college dropout who works as a clerk in his family's kitschy lingerie store and dreams of evading the national economic crisis by moving to Europe—if he could only save enough money for airfare.

Fabián Bielinsky's *Nine Queens* is another paradigm of urban film in the midst of *corralito*, the colloquial name for the economic measures taken in Argentina at the end of 2001 that almost completely froze bank accounts and

forbade withdrawals. The witty story of two swindlers in corrupt Buenos Aires who meet by chance and decide to team up for a scam, it's a hectic excursion from one side of the Argentine capital to the other. The film concludes with a memorable scene in which the luxurious **Hilton Hotel**, located in the recently renovated neighborhood of **Puerto Madero**, provides the backdrop for the sale of some counterfeit stamps, called "The Nine Queens," to a rich Spaniard. The film did well at the U.S. box office and was later remade as an English-language film by Gregory Jacobs.

Jorge Luis Borges once defined the relationship between Argentina and her citizens as "dread and love." And the ambivalence described by him is present everywhere in current Argentine filmography. This is not a metaphor: Borges was talking about both the kind of dread that wakes people in the night with nightmares of starvation and the colossal love that leads two street kids to wonder if the Obelisco can be the biggest sex symbol of the world. §

Andrea Chignoli is a Chilean film editor and film professor, who has lived in Cuba, New York, Buenos Aires and Chile.

---

^ *Nine Queens*, 2000. photo: ©FX Sound/Everett Collection
‹ **Puerto Madero** photo: ©Eduardo Rivero
[next page] **Chilean vineyard** photo: ©Tim Abbott

08

BEFORE AND AFTER TYRANNY

CHILE

ALVARO CEPPI
Most memorable experience in film/travel: Spending New Year's Eve 2003 at the Aragon Ballroom in Chicago for a double feature of the White Stripes and the Flaming Lips–two of my favorite bands. Watching them playing *"Seven Nation Army"* together at midnight was unforgettable.

• Central Valley

Valparaiso •
Tunquen • Santiago
Isla Negra

During the 17 years Chile suffered under the repressive rule of its last dictator, Augusto Pinochet, cinema was almost nonexistent. But with the arrival of democracy in the '90s, the art scene, like a rusty machine oiled back into life, hatched a whole new generation of filmmakers. (It's hard to call this movement an outright industry when just 10 to 12 movies are premiering each year.) Around this time, offerings like the real-life heist film *Johnny 100 Pesos*—a 1994 Sundance Film Festival crowd pleaser and critical favorite—ushered in a cynical view of a society still traumatized by violence in everyday life.

SANTIAGO

Pesos, directed by Gustavo Graef-Marino, takes place in the capital city, located in Chile's central valley. The tumultuous locale and its 5.5 million dwellers (give or take) have provided a backdrop for many features in the 100-plus years of the country's film history—from the 1903 short documentary *Ejercicio general de bombas*, which showed firemen training at **Anibal Pinto Square**, to director Andrés Wood's *La buena vida (The Good Life)*, a movie about the modern-day struggles in Santiago. Wood explored the 1973 military coup there with *Machuca* (2004), and his *Good Life* also takes place in the city, exploring downtown Santiago's most iconic sites. Among them: the **cafe con piernas** (or "legged coffee shop") establishments, a Hooters for the java crowd where male clerks and office workers down espressos served by scantily clad, stiletto-heeled waitresses. Crude? Possibly, but these shops are also healthy markers of a liberated Chilean society embracing sexual *destape* (literally, "to uncover"), a phenomenon similar to the cultural shift seen in the post-Franco Spain of the late '70s or in '80s Argentina following its period of military dictatorship.

Before socialist Salvador Allende was elected president in 1970, Santiago actually boasted quite the bohemian nightlife, which was reflected in cinema such as Raúl Ruiz's 1968 drama *Tres tristes tigres*. (The acclaimed director would later change his first name to Raoul when he fled the country after the 1973 coup; he's been living in Paris since.) The title of the film, a Spanish tongue twister, translates into "three sad tigers," a metaphor for the trio of petty-bourgeois protagonists who hang out in bars, unable to face the changing political realities of the time. Three years later Ruiz made

‹ **Santiago, Chile** photo: ©kwest

Palomita Blanca (Little White Dove), a romance about social clashes at the end of the '60s. In the movie, an uptown boy and lower-class girl fall in love amid a classic Santiago setting: the **Providencia District**, Chile's equivalent of London's hip Carnaby Street. The two protagonists, María and Juan Carlos, meet up at the **Drugstore**, a small Providencia shopping center. This mall remains in business, offering a wide selection of local designers' wares in its stores and small coffee shops where patrons drink a *cortado* (café latte) while reading the daily paper or chatting with friends.

Patricio Guzmán's documentary *La batalla de Chile* (The Battle of Chile), meanwhile, took the best snapshot of the Allende/pre-Pinochet era that followed—a chilling image of a country in flux, prefiguring the slaughter to come. One scene depicts the government house, **Palacio de la Moneda**, being bombed by the Chilean Air Force. Another finds cameraman Hans Herman, an Argentine, filming the army insurrection close to la Moneda on September 11, 1973; in a tragic twist, he ended up capturing his own death. The footage shows gun-wielding soldiers aiming at the camera, which stays in focus until Herman is hit and the image spins out of control.

After the return of democracy in the '90s, the blocks around la Moneda, and the building itself, were completely restored. Nearby, the reestablished **Plaza de la Ciudadanía** (Citizenry Square) included a new Cultural Center called Centro Cultural Palacio la Moneda. The arts also benefited from state help in the post-Pinochet eras. The popular 2001 film *Taxi para tres (A Cab for Three)*, for instance, was made thanks to a grant. This *Collateral*-esque story from Orlando Lübbert focuses on a cab driver harassed by a pair of small-time crooks: They give him the option of driving them around town during a crime spree or spending that time locked up in the trunk. Guess which way he went? The movie takes place in the dry landscape of Santiago's poorer western neighborhoods as well as downtown Santiago's main square, the **Plaza de Armas**, where the thugs declaim against the local slang while eating *churrascos chacareros* sandwiches.

For a very different view of the city, turn to 2005's *Play*, directed by newcomer Alicia Scherson. In the drama, a young man and woman fruitlessly search for love while unwittingly crossing paths. The characters move from the traditional area of **Old Santiago** (the **Barrio Brasil** students' quarter) to the **Las Condes** uptown, a neighborhood of shopping malls and SUVs resembling an American suburb. The latter location is likewise

where Matías Bize's *Sábado (Saturday)* was shot. This 60-minute-long experimental picture from 2003, about the travails of a woman who discovers her fiancé is cheating on her, was reportedly shot with a digital camera on a budget of just 2,500 pesos (or $50).

VALPARAÍSO

Head eight miles out of Santiago, and you'll find this port city—which boasts a labyrinth of narrow streets and cobblestone alleyways—built upon dozens of steep hillsides overlooking the Pacific Ocean. Aldo Francia, a pediatrician-turned-filmmaker, used this deceivingly beauteous setting for his 1968 neo-realistic drama *Valparaíso Mi Amor*, about a family that drifts into delinquency and prostitution after its patriarch lands in prison for robbery. Valeria Sarmiento also set her 1990 film, *Amelia López O'Neill*, in the picturesque environs. Though not as gritty as Francia's take, Sarmiento's vision certainly is harrowing: it's the tale of a well-bred young woman who remains faithful to the doctor who deflowers her, even after he marries her invalid sister. That same year, upon Chile's return to democracy, Silvio Caiozzi released his Valparaíso-set movie, *La luna en el espejo (The Moon in the Mirror)*. It, too, is an unsettling tale—about a possessive, tyrannical retired naval officer who lives with his long-suffering unmarried son.

TUNQUEN

This charming little fishing village lies sixty kilometers down from Valparaíso, and it's where Sebastián Campos' 2005 film *La sagrada familia (The Sacred Family)* was shot. The sex- and drug-fueled movie follows the slow disintegration of an apparently normal family over the Easter holidays.

ISLA NEGRA

Another little coastal town near Valparaíso, Isla Negra is best known as the *setting* for Antonio Skármeta's **Ardiente paciencia** *(Burning Patience)*, since the film was actually shot in Portugal. Why visit? The movie tells the story of a poor postman who befriends Chilean poet Pablo Neruda—his old residence, now the **Neruda Museum**, still stands on the stunning isle—and asks him to help write a few potent

^ *Il Postino*, 1994. photo: ©Blue Dahlia Productions/Everett Collection
> **Valparaiso** photo: ©Happy Alex
[next page] **Easter Island** photo: ©Happy Alex

verses to seduce a woman; this plot that was later recycled for the 1994 international hit *Il Postino*.

OTHER PARTS OF THE CENTRAL VALLEY

One of Chile's first feature-length films—the 1925 guerrilla drama *El húsar de la muerte (The Hussar of Death)*, directed by Pedro Sienna—takes place in this lush, agricultural land of Chile's **Central Valley**. Ensconced between two mountain ranges, the area is considered an oenophile's dream—and a sound investment, seeing as how generations of wealthy clans continue to lay claim to much of this region. Director Silvio Caiozzi took a peek into their world with his 1977 movie, *Julio comienza en Julio (Julio Begins in July)*, about an affluent Chilean landowner who celebrates his son's 15th birthday with a delegation of local prostitutes; plans go awry when the boy falls in love with one of the working girls.

Perhaps the most remarkable thing about the Chilean film world (other than producing a legitimately good movie about a dad re-creating Sodom for his underage son, of course) is its resilience. With a landscape that could make Hollywood drool and a talent pool that rivals some of indie filmmaking's best, Chile now also has an open-minded government, eager to inject cash into this ever-evolving scene. Film buffs from around the world can now appreciate the thought-provoking artistry that such liberty—free of both militant leaders and capitalist trappings—has encouraged. §

Alvaro Ceppi is a filmmaker who's directed more than 40 music videos for various Chilean acts. In 2002, along with three partners, he formed Sólo por las Niñas Audiovisual (Only for the Girls AV), an animation and live action studio. Their works include two animated TV shows, *Block!* and *Experimento Wayapolis*, which Ceppi wrote and directed. Both shows won Chilean Television Council Fund Awards. People of the world can see their work at www.spln.cl

< **Aconcagua Mountain** photo: ©Jason Maehl
[next page] **Vancouver Public Library** photo: ©Fred Goldstein

READING / VIEWING
APPENDIX

SUGGESTED READING/VIEWING

Though not in major distribution, Museyon Guides acknowledges and highly recommends contacting the director himself for a copy of *Los Angeles Plays Itself*, a video essay about Los Angeles as the capital of on-location filming. Director Thom Anderson is a professor at the California Institute of Arts.

http://www.filminamerica.com/

http://www.gildasattic.com/Greed.html

http://www.filmsite.org/

http://www.rjsmith.com/bullitt-locations.html

http://cinemareview.com/production.asp?prodid=3799

Footsteps in the Fog: Alfred Hitchcock's San Francisco, 2002. Kraft, Jeff. Leventhal, Aaron. Santa Monica: Santa Monica Press

INDEX + CREDITS
FILM

FILM	YEAR	DVD DISTRIBUTOR	CHAPTER	PAGE
Crash	1996	Lions Gate	Canada	120
Crimes of the Future	1970	n/a	Canada	120
Crocodile Dundee	1986	Paramount	NYC	37
Cronos	1993	Lions Gate	Mexico	74
Dark Passage	1947	Warner	San Francisco	13
Dawson's Creek	1998	Sony	The South	61
Day After Tomorrow, The	2004	20th Century Fox	Canada	114
Deliverance	1972	Warner	The South	58
Desperately Seeking Susan	1985	MGM	NYC	29
Devil Wears Prada, The	2006	20th Century Fox	NYC	37
Dirty Dancing 2: Havana Nights	2004	Lions Gate	Puerto Rico	92
Dirty Harry	1971	Warner	San Francisco	16
Driving Miss Daisy	1989	Warner	The South	49
Divine Secrets of the Ya-Ya Sisterhood, The	2002	Warner	The South	61
Dog, The	2004	Cameo	Argentina	135
Dune	1984	Universal	Mexico	74
Ejercicio General de Bombas	1903	n/a	Chile	145
El bonaerense	2002	Optimum Home Ent	Argentina	135
El perro	2004	n/a	Argentina	135
Evita	1996	Hollywood Pictures Home Video	Argentina	127
Fantasma	2006	n/a	Argentina	138
Fantastic Four: Rise of the Silver Surfer	2007	20th Century Fox	Canada	110
Final Destination 3	2006	New Line	Canada	110
Forrest Gump	1994	Paramount	The South	55
Fountain, The	2007	Warner	Canada	114
Four Brothers	2005	Paramount	Canada	119
Frida	2002	Miramax	Mexico	74
Fried Green Tomatoes	1991	Universal	The South	61
FUBAR	2002	Xenon	Canada	113
Gatica, el Mono	1993	n/a	Argentina	132
Ghostbusters	1984	Columbia	NYC	31
Glory	1989	Columbia	The South	52

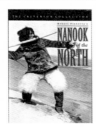

FILM	YEAR	DVD DISTRIBUTOR	CHAPTER	PAGE
Palomita Blanca	1976	n/a	Chile	147
Patriot, The	2000	Sony	The South	55
Pizza, Beer, Smokes	1999	n/a	Argentina	127
Play	2005	n/a	Chile	147
Play It Again, Sam	1972	Paramount	San Francisco	25
Prince of Tides, The	1991	Sony	The South	58
Pursuit of Happyness, The	2006	Sony	San Francisco	22
Rapado	1992	n/a	Argentina	127
Resident Evil: Apocalypse	2004	Sony Pictures	Canada	119
River of No Return	1954	20th Century Fox	Canada	110
Road to San Diego, The	2006	n/a	Argentina	135
Rolling Family	2004	Palm Pictures	Argentina	135
Romeo + Juliet	1996	20th Century Fox	Mexico	74
Rosemary's Baby	1968	Paramount	NYC	37
Rowdyman, The	1972	n/a	Canada	120
Roxanne	1987	Sony	Canada	110
Royal Tenenbaums, The	2001	Paramount	NYC	40
Sacred Family, The	2005	n/a	Chile	150
Saskatchewan	1954	Filmax	Canada	110
Saturday	2001	Cinemateca	Chile	150
Scooby Doo 2: Monsters Unleashed	2004	Warner	Canada	110
Score, The	2001	Paramount	Canada	114
Secret Life of Bees, The	2008	n/a	The South	61
Sentinel, The	2007	Universal	Canada	119
Seven Year Itch, The	1955	20th Century Fox	NYC	34
Sex and the City	2008	New Line	NYC	34
Shaft	1971	Warner	NYC	31
Sharkey's Machine	1981	Warner	The South	49
Shipping News, The	2001	Miramax	Canada	120
Silver Streak	1976	20th Century Fox	Canada	119
Sister Act	1992	Touchstone	San Francisco	25
Sixth Day, The	2000	Sony	Canada	110
Skidoo	1968	n/a	San Francisco	22
South, The	1988	n/a	Argentina	129
Steel Magnolias	1989	Sony	The South	61

FILM	YEAR	DVD DISTRIBUTOR	CHAPTER	PAGE
Stereo	1969	n/a	Canada	120
Strange Brew	1983	Warner Bros.	Canada	114
Streetcar Named Desire, A	1951	Warner	The South	47
Suburbanators, The	1995	Troma Ent	Canada	110
Superman 3	1983	Warner Bros.	Canada	110
Swamp, The	2001	Home Vision Ent	Argentina	132
Taxi Driver	1976	Sony	NYC	34
Taxi para tres	2001	Maverick	Chile	147
Thieves Like Us	1974	MGM Video	The South	61
Tideland	2005	Velocity	Canada	110
Time to Kill, A	1996	Warner	The South	61
Titanic	1997	Paramount	Mexico	74
Towering Inferno, The	1974	20th Century Fox	San Francisco	22
Traffic	2000	Universal	Mexico	77
Tres tristes tigres	1968	n/a	Chile	145
Undercover Brother	2002	Universal	Canada	114
Unforgiven	1992	Warner	Canada	107
Valparaiso mi amor	1968	n/a	Chile	150
Vertigo	1958	Universal	San Francisco	16
Warriors, The	1979	Paramount	NYC	43
waydowntown	2000	Homevision	Canada	113
When the Levees Broke	2006	HBO Home Ent	The South	49
William Shakespeare's Romeo + Juliet	1996	20th Century Fox	Mexico	80
X-Men	2000	20th Century Fox	Canada	119
XXY	2007	Film Movement	Argentina	135
Y Tu Mama Tambien	2002	MGM	Mexico	69
Zodiac	2007	Paramount	San Francisco	16
Zoolander	2001	Paramount	NYC	31

ABOUT MUSEYON GUIDES

Museyon: A Curated Guide to Your Obsessions is a guide book series that gives the curious subject a new and differently informed look at their interests. Based out of New York City with origins in Tokyo, Paris, and just about everywhere in between, Museyon is an independent publisher of quality information.

ABOUT THE ILLUSTRATOR

 Jillian Tamaki is an illustrator from Calgary, Alberta who now lives in Brooklyn, NY. In addition to her myriad editorial illustrations for publications such as *Entertainment Weekly, The New York Times,* and *SPIN,* she is also an award-winning graphic novelist. Co-authored along with her cousin Mariko Tamaki, *Skim* was released in March 2008 and received the Ignatz Award for Best Graphic Novel.

Most memorable film/travel experience: While driving around Iceland, we got snowed in at the very top of the island, in a city called Akureyri. To while away the time, we hit the local theatre which was playing the film *Stardust,* part of which happened to be filmed in Iceland. The mossy green hills were instantly recognizable and the people in the theatre were quite amused, pointing and chuckling. It was very strange to be in a movie theatre near the Arctic Circle, and even stranger to see the landscape we'd been moving through for the last week up on the screen.

ACKNOWLEDGEMENTS

Photography for the Museyon Guides has been graciously provided by dozens of citizen photographers found through Flickr.com, and Museyon would like to thank them, as well as istockphoto.com and shutterstock.com.

Photo Editor/Contributor: Michael Kuhle (28)

flickr: 24, 30, 35, 36, 41, 59, 66, 68, 70, 75, 78, 79, 81, 82, 82, 90, 93, 99, 100, 111, 139, 146

istockphoto: 14, 17, 18, 26, 42, 54, 64, 76, 86, 94, 96, 136, 142, 148

shutterstock: 8, 10, 12, 17, 20, 23, 32, 38, 44, 46, 48, 50, 53, 56, 60, 84, 88, 93, 102, 104, 106, 108, 112, 115, 116, 118, 121, 122, 124, 126, 128, 30, 133, 134, 140, 144, 151, 152, 154

Everett Collection: 11, 16, 22, 29, 40, 47, 58, 74, 80, 87, 98, 107, 120, 127

Every effort has been made to trace and compensate copyright holders, and we apologize in advance for any accidental omissions. We will be happy to apply the corrections in the following editions of this publication.

18·95